Heart to Heart

A Mother-Daughter Devotional With 50 Devotions for Teen Girls

By Teen Daughter & Mother Coauthors

Bekah and Stacey Pardoe

Praise for *Heart to Heart*

I wish I could have read this book as a teenager. Instead of slamming doors I could have been learning more constructive ways to express my feelings. Every mom and teenage daughter need this book in order to open those lines of communication without the awkwardness that comes when trying to have those hard conversations face to face. With this interactive journal a bond between mother and daughter can bloom.

Brianna Barrett, *writer at briannagrams.com*

Heart to Heart is an interactive and heartwarming book to help mothers and daughters navigate the tender high school years together. Stacey's heart and vision is to help mothers and daughters deeply connect as they read and reflect on the different challenges most teens face in a gentle, encouraging way. I love how they include in each day a focus verse and devotional with plenty of space for both daughter and mom to reflect and respond. I wish I had access to this devotional when my two girls were in high school.

Donna Miller, *writer at freshgracefortoday.com*

Heart to Heart is the devotional I needed as a teen girl, and it is a treasured guide as I navigate an unexpected motherly role with my fifteen-year-old niece. Stacey and Bekah invite you to create a safe space through a journaling experience that encourages open communication and nurtures an intimate relationship with the teenage girl in your life. Each day, you will discuss life challenges and dreams relevant to young ladies in today's world and expose them to Biblical truth, prayer, and experiential wisdom in a way that fosters and grows a relationship with each other and, most importantly, with Christ. This book is a much-needed tool for any woman in a supportive role who desires to connect on a deeper level.

Darcie Fuqua, *Youth Director, speaker, mental health advocate, and writer at leightonlane.com*

Are you looking to connect with your teenage daughter in a meaningful and spiritually impactful way? The amazing mother/daughter duo, Stacey and Bekah Pardoe, are back again with another mom and daughter devotional that will provoke deep thoughts, promote spiritual conversation, and provide a way for you and your teen to share in God's purposes for her life. My daughter and I have been blessed by both *Girl to Girl* and now *Heart to Heart*.

Arrica Hess, *writer at achildshallleadthemblog.com*

Heart to Heart is a beautifully written mother-daughter devotional for teen girls. Stacey's simplicity, openness and vulnerability in writing always help her audience connect deeply with her words. In this devotional, she draws from her own experiences as a teenager and mom to inspire and challenge teenage girls as they navigate the sometimes troubled waters of teenage years. Stacey shares deep-rooted wisdom as she gives godly perspective to different subjects that teenage girls will face, even the most difficult topics like sex and forgiveness. This book will help moms and daughters to connect on a deep level, kickstart meaningful conversations and also share life experiences.

I recommend this mom-daughter devotional to every mom who seeks to bond intimately with her child and desires that her daughter learns to bring God into her everyday experiences.

Ufuoma Fijabi, author of Dear Mother: 12 Quiet Reflections from a Mother's Heart; co-author of 30 Prophetic Prayers and Declarations to Speak Over Your Child; and writer at oneinspiredmum.com

Table of Contents

Let's Connect!

When I was a teenager, I longed for faith that was strong enough to carry me through the challenges I was facing. I needed faith that would sustain me through breakups, give me peace in stressful times, help me overcome my fears, and provide confidence as I made important decisions.

I tried reading my Bible but often felt overwhelmed by the sheer volume and confusing details in it. My prayer life mostly consisted of asking God for help in difficult situations. I also felt awkward reaching out to older believers for advice.

Asking my parents to help me deal with the temptations I was facing—and the mistakes I was making—was embarrassing. I had a few older friends who offered guidance, but I often felt like I was just trying to survive my teen years.

By the grace of God, I survived.

Now that I'm a parent, I have a deep desire to help my kids navigate their teen years with as much support as possible. I hope to help them connect with God in ways that impact their everyday moments. I want to support them as they step into a kind of faith that's strong enough to carry them through shattered dreams, heartbreaking losses, and devastating mistakes.

When our daughter, Bekah, became a teenager, connecting became challenging. We were both busy. Bekah was pulled in dozens of different directions with school, sports, friendships, and other activities. I was trying to work, care for our family, and do all the mysterious things moms do.

Additionally, connecting was challenging because it's not always easy to talk about tough issues. Talking about dating, the pressure to fit in, and other awkward topics felt uncomfortable. At times, we struggled to communicate clearly.

Because I am a writer, I did what writer-moms do: I wrote a book for my daughter. I wrote about the challenges I faced as a teenager and created a journaling section where Bekah and I could both reflect on our lives. My vision was to create a safe space where Bekah and I could share our hearts about important topics. I also hoped to create a space where she knew she could open up to me without judgment or the discomfort of trying to talk about awkward issues face-to-face.

After sharing the devotional with Bekah, she asked if she could add a few devotions of her own, making it a mother-daughter devotional to help other moms and daughters. I agreed, and this book came to life. We're excited to share our hearts with you.

How to Use This Devotional Journal

Our vision is that teen girls and their moms will use this devotional journal together and find space for connecting within these pages. We also understand that not all teens and parents have strong relationships. For this reason, we wrote it in such a way that any older mentor can work through these writings with a teen. The mentor might be a grandparent, aunt, uncle, youth leader, teacher, coach, counselor, neighbor, or even an older sibling or friend.

Using the book is simple. Each daily reading begins with a Focus Verse that sets the stage for the day's reading, followed by a devotional reflection written by one of us. You might choose to read the daily devotions together, or you might choose to read them in your own time.

Following each daily reading, you will find a few reflective questions for the teen to write about as well as a space for Mom's response. The teen will write her responses first, in her own time. Mom should respond afterward and offer insights into her daughter's reflections alongside her own reflections. When Bekah and I use a shared journal, we leave the journal on one another's beds after writing.

Girls, we encourage you to be as honest as possible when you write your journal entries. This isn't a time to sugarcoat your struggles. See it as an opportunity to open up about the troubles you're dealing with, ask questions about your faith, share your worries, and be honest about the temptations you're facing.

Moms, we'll share a few pointers for you after Bekah introduces herself. First, here's Bekah!

A Note From Bekah

Hey! I'm Bekah, and I'm so happy you're here with us. Before we start, let me tell you a bit more about myself. I'm a teenage girl who's into things like art, animals, and hanging out with my friends.

When people introduce themselves, they usually talk about everything they like, but I think you can learn about a person by what they *dislike*, too. My dislikes include going to school (it majorly stresses me out!) and getting into trouble. I don't get into tons of trouble, but my parents get on my case about how awful my room sometimes looks, talking back, and fighting with my two younger brothers.

You can also learn a lot about a person from their hobbies. I love creating artwork and taking care of animals. I also run cross country and am a distance runner on the track team. As I write this to you today, I've been getting up at the crack of dawn to run with my cross country team all summer, and as much as I like the sport, I wish I didn't have to get up so early to do it!

All in all, I'd say I live a pretty normal life. I face the same struggles you probably face—things like school stress, exhaustion, disappointment, loneliness, and frustration. We'll be talking about some of these issues together in this book.

I hope you have a great time reading this devotional, and I pray it helps you grow with God. I hope that the experiences my mom and I share within these pages help you know that you're not alone. Sometimes, we all feel alone in life—especially as teenagers—but we are never truly alone. Other people understand and have experienced similar struggles. Most of all, God understands, and he promises to walk with each of us through every trial we face in life.

That's all from me for now!

Just for Mom (From Stacey)

Hey, Mom. Before we get started, I want to thank you for caring about your daughter and seeking a closer relationship. As you journey together through this book, remember that your primary goal is to make this a safe space for her to be honest.

I encourage you to approach this book with the mindset that nothing your daughter shares will offend you or push you away. Teens need safe spaces where they can open up without the fear of judgment or rejection.

As you create a secure space for your daughter to talk about challenging topics, rest assured that you don't need to have all of the right answers. More than anything, your daughter needs to know that you care about her struggles and that you are on her side to support her—no matter what. Also, remember to keep the words she shares confidential.

Additionally, I encourage you to pray, pray, and keep on praying! Pray for your daughter every day. The fact that she is willing to do this devotional with you is a sign that God is working in her heart. When you open this book, before reading her journal entries, pray. Ask God to allow you to read between the lines, to see what your daughter is sharing indirectly.

Before you write your responses, pray again. Ask the Holy Spirit to direct your words and give you the specific encouragement your daughter needs to read. Do your best to respond in a way that doesn't come across as "preachy." Instead, begin by sharing the ways you relate to her questions, doubts, temptations, and failures. Let her know that she's not alone. Show her that you get it. Offer some practical advice but be careful not to be at all condemning.

Lastly, this devotional journal is designed to be a springboard for face-to-face conversations about the topics addressed within these pages. Think of it as a way to get the ball rolling.

When you do bring up a topic for conversation, if your daughter shuts down or doesn't want to talk about it, respect that boundary. Also, be careful to talk about these topics in private for the sake of confidentiality. Bekah and I like to hike together, and I try to wait until we're in the woods before addressing private or difficult topics.

Most of all, have fun with this.

When appropriate, weave humor into your written responses. Let this be a time to grow closer together and build the foundation of a relationship that will last for decades.

Thank you for taking this journey with us. We pray that God uses it to move mountains!

Day 1

The Fear of Failure

And not only this, but we also celebrate in our tribulations, knowing that tribulation brings about perseverance; and perseverance, proven character; and proven character, hope.

Romans 5:3-4

When I was 16, I failed in a disappointing and slightly embarrassing way. I failed my driving test.

On the day of my driving test, I aced the written part of the exam, breezed through the driving portion, and proceeded to smash into the curb *three* times while attempting to parallel park. To this day, I don't understand why parallel parking is a prerequisite for acquiring a driver's license in our state.

As a result of my failure, I walked out of the DMV with my head held low. A day that was supposed to be an exciting gateway into my almost-adult life turned out to be a huge disappointment.

I now realize that failing a driving test is a relatively small mishap. Nevertheless, my 16-year-old brain told me that the failure was *monumental*. For seven long days, I lamented over my failure, at which point, I was given a second chance, parallel parked like a pro, and walked away with my license.

I share this story with you today because it offers an important reminder.

We all fail.

We all fall short. Failing while undertaking endeavors that are important to us can be crushing. In these times, it's helpful to remind ourselves that failure is an essential part of growth.

I spent most of my teens and twenties doing everything within my power to avoid failure. Over time, I realized that the fear of failure often kept me from taking necessary risks.

When I shared this realization with a mentor, he offered advice that went something like this: "Stacey, the world will tell you to run from even the possibility of failure. However, Jesus modeled a life of embracing failure. He wasn't afraid of appearing foolish, being rejected, or losing popularity. Learning to embrace failure—and the growth that comes through it—is an important part of following Christ."

Since that time, I have learned not to run from experiences in which my probability of failing is high. Instead, when I sense God leading me, I move toward these experiences because I know that they will help me become more like Christ and grow in maturity.

Share any experiences with failure that came to mind as you read this devotion. How do you typically respond when you face a situation in which you know you might fail? Do you move toward or away from the possibility of failure? Do you currently sense God asking you to step into anything you've been putting off due to the fear of failure?

____

____

____

____

____

____

____

____

____

____

____

____

Mom's Reflection

After responding to your daughter's reflection, describe a time when God used a personal failure to help you grow. What did this experience teach you about failure, or how did it reframe your perspective?

____

____

____

____

____

____

____

Day 2

De-Stress With God

Come to Me, all who are weary and burdened, and I
will give you rest.

Matthew 11:28

What's stressing you out the most right now? You might be
dealing with conflict in a friendship, trying to get over a
breakup, praying you pass a difficult class, or worrying
about your future plans.

We all face stress. As time passes, our stressors change,
but they never go away. For this reason, learning to unload
your burdens with God is life-changing.

As a teenager, I was almost always stressed out over
homework, tests, and grades. I was also an athlete, which
meant that I dealt with the stress of juggling sports, school,
and relationships. At other times, I faced stress over
disagreements within friendships, important decisions,
dating, and more.

Over time, I learned that I needed to regularly create
space to de-stress with God. I often walked to the woods
behind my parents' house, sat on a hill overlooking a vast
expanse of farmland, and sorted through my troubles with
God.

Sometimes, I wrote in my journal. At other times, I read my Bible or copied verses into a notebook. Often, I simply shared my troubles with God as if I were talking to my best friend. I told him everything I was feeling and asked him to help me process my emotions. I rarely experienced life-changing revelations from God as I sat in the woods; yet I always returned home feeling lighter—as if a burden had been lifted.

Years later, I still process my emotions with God while spending time outdoors. In the evenings, I often take long walks in the valley behind our house. I sort through my worries, share my burdens with God, and create space to rest with him. These moments are restorative and refreshing.

God wants you to learn to de-stress with him, too. You might not be into spending time in nature, but I encourage you to find a place where you can be alone with God and share your burdens with him. You might close your bedroom door, listen to music, and talk to God while you lie on your bed. Some people like to connect with God while they drive, exercise, or create artwork.

Today's Focus Verse tells us that when we bring our burdens to Jesus, he gives us rest. God wants to help you work through stress and lift your burdens, too. Remember that he is ready and waiting to help you. He is inviting you to draw near to him and receive his rest.

Teen's Reflection

What is stressing you out the most right now? What have you been doing to cope with the stress? If you were sitting with Jesus and telling him about this worry, what do you think he'd say to you? Where could you go to regularly de-stress with God?

____

____

____

____

____

____

____

____

____

____

____

____

____

____

Mom's Reflection

After reading your daughter's reflection above, in what ways can you relate to these stressors and worries? Where do you go when you need to de-stress with God? Share any insights that might help your daughter learn to de-stress with God.

____

____

____

____

____

Day 3

Your Closest Friends

A cord of three strands is not quickly torn apart.

Ecclesiastes 4:12

Take a moment to think about your closest friends. What do you like to do together for fun? What characteristics do you appreciate about these friends?

Today's Focus Verse tells us that a chord of three strands isn't easily broken. When it comes to relationships, these three strands refer to you, your friend, and an unexpected third strand: Jesus.

Have you ever noticed that it's hard to break a braided chord? When Jesus is present in your friendships, similar to three-stranded chords, these friendships are stronger.

Every year around Christmas, I get together with a handful of friends I've known since we were kids. We catch up on our lives, tell old stories, laugh together, and encourage one another.

It's remarkable that we've been friends for so many years. As I reflect on these friendships, I notice a common thread: We are all followers of Christ.

I can't help but think that being united by the three-stranded chord of faith in Christ has helped us remain connected over the years. At times, we go for months without any contact. Nevertheless, I've learned that when hard times come, I can count on these friends.

They show up on my doorstep with food when crises strike, and they offer comfort when I feel discouraged. When I doubt my faith or wrestle with difficult questions, they remind me of God's Truth and help me find healing in his presence.

It's healthy to have friends who are believers as well as friends who aren't. However, if you don't have any close Christian friends, ask God to bring some into your life.

These friends can help you in your walk with God and point you to the Truth in challenging times.

Teen's Reflection

Do you have any close Christian friends? In what ways are these friendships different than your friendships with those who don't believe? Do you find it difficult or easy to connect with other Christians? Why do you think this is so?

____

____

____

____

Mom's Reflection

What encouragement can you offer your daughter when it comes to pursuing relationships with Christian friends? Also, share your life experience with friendships: In what ways have your Christian friends helped, supported, and encouraged you? Why are these friends important to you?

____

____

____

____

____

____

____

____

____

Day 4

Can I Mess up God's Plan for My Life?

Your ears will hear a word behind you, saying, "This is the way, walk in it," whenever you turn to the right or to the left.

Isaiah 30:21

I've spent far too much time worrying that I might somehow mess up God's plans for my life. In high school, I was afraid of choosing the wrong sport or taking classes that were too hard: I didn't want to derail my future by playing basketball if I was supposed to be training for track. I was afraid that taking advanced classes would hurt my GPA, take away my chances for earning scholarships, and totally ruin my life.

Dramatic, I know.

My fears amplified when it was time to choose a college and declare a major. I vividly remember thinking, *How are teenagers supposed to know what they want to do with their adult lives?* (I still wrestle with this question, and my heart goes out to you!)

Ultimately, God showed me that I didn't need to be afraid of messing up my life. He showed me that as long as I did my best to seek him and make wise decisions, he would be faithful to redirect me every time I stepped off the best path for my life.

I've veered off that path plenty of times, and God has always been faithful to pick me up and redirect me. I've learned that as long as I do my best to seek and follow him, God is faithful to lead and guide me.

God will be faithful to you, too. Aim to follow him. Make the best decisions you can make with the knowledge you have right now. Then, trust that God will guide you and redirect you when necessary. He is faithful!

Teen's Reflection

How do you feel when you look to the future? What feels uncertain? What feels hopeful? What are you most afraid of? In what way would you like God to guide you as you prepare to step into the future?

____

____

____

____

____

____

____

____

____

____

____

____

____

____

____

____

Mom's Reflection

After reading and responding to your daughter's reflection, take a moment to remember how it felt to be a teenager looking ahead to an uncertain future. What would you tell your teenage self about trusting God's sovereignty over your life? What have you learned about God's faithfulness?

Day 5

Teen to Teen With Bekah

Your True Identity

For I am convinced that neither death, nor life,
nor angels, nor principalities, nor things present, nor
things to come, nor powers, nor height, nor depth, nor
any other created thing will be able to separate us
from the love of God that is in Christ Jesus our Lord.

Romans 8:38-39

We all find our identities in various ways. This might include deciding who we are based on what we like to do for fun, how we dress, and our talents.

My favorite activities are running, drawing, watching shows, writing, and hanging out with friends. I could name countless more, but that would take *all* day.

These parts of our identities are subject to change over time. For example, when I was younger, I didn't hang out with my friends nearly as often as I do now. Other things have changed, too. I don't dress the way I did when I was younger, and many of my interests have changed.

Maybe you can relate. If you reflect on the past few years, many things have probably changed.

You might be wondering what I'm getting at here.

Well, I have a question for you: Do you know the one part of your identity that will never change?

The answer is this: You will always be loved by God.

No matter how much you change, God will always love you. Nothing can break his unending love for you.

Think about it. Adam and Eve completely betrayed God's trust. He still loved them. The Apostle Paul persecuted Christians. God loved him so much that he pursued him and changed his heart. The Israelites turned away from God and worshiped false gods. And you know what? God still loved them.

You can put your faith in God.

He will always love you—no matter what.

The truest part of your identity is that you are loved by God. There is *nothing* you could ever do to cause God to love you less or lead him to stop loving you.

Learn to stand on the truth of your unchanging identity as God's deeply loved child, and you won't need to prove yourself to others. You won't be desperate to fit in or impress others. God will set you free to love others in a way that is pure and true. His love will flow through you, and you will find peace and freedom.

Teen's Reflection

Take a moment to reflect and describe yourself using three words. After listing these words, consider whether these three words might no longer describe you later in life. In what ways would your life be different if you truly grasped the depth of God's unchanging love for you? Which area of your life would be the most impacted by the power of God's love?

Mom's Reflection

If you could describe your teenage self using three words, what words would you choose? Now, if you were to describe your current self using three words, what words would you choose? In what ways has God's love transformed your life? Share any reflections about the freedom you have experienced as you've embraced God's love for you.

____

____

____

____

____

____

____

____

____

Day 6

Life's Closed Doors

Trust in the Lord with all your heart and do not lean
on your own understanding. In all your ways
acknowledge Him, and He will make your paths
straight.

Proverbs 3:5-6

A few years ago, a dream I'd been chasing for a long time fell to pieces. I thought I'd found my dream job, but the job didn't work out. It felt like a door had been slammed shut in my face—so hard that it knocked me down.

Has God ever closed a door in your face?

Maybe you were trying out for a team or hoping to get a role in a performance. Perhaps you didn't make it onto the homecoming court, into the club you wanted to join, or into the college you hoped to attend. Maybe your boyfriend broke up with you and broke your heart.

These rejections are devastating.

I've faced many of them, too.

I've also learned an important life lesson through these disappointments: God often closes doors for our protection.

When God closed the door on my dream job several years ago, I had no idea that he was protecting me from walking down a path that wasn't best for me.

As he redirected me, he led me to pursue a new dream that was exponentially more fulfilling than the first dream ever could have been. I am forever grateful that God didn't let me venture down the wrong path—a path that wasn't a part of his perfect plan for me.

When God closes a door in your life, you can trust that he has a better plan for you. It often takes time for his better plan to reveal itself. In the meantime, he is able to work all things for good. While you wait, God invites you trust to him with the parts of your life that don't make sense to you. He has not stopped working.

Teen's Reflection

What part of your life doesn't make sense to you right now? Has God closed any doors recently? Write about this experience and reflect on how God might be inviting you to grow in trust while you wait on him.

____

____

____

____

____

____

____

____

____

____

____

____

____

Mom's Reflection

After prayerfully responding to your daughter's thoughts, describe a time when God closed a door of opportunity in your life—particularly, a time when the closed door felt disappointing. In what ways did God use this closed door to protect you or lead you into a better plan?

____

____

____

____

____

____

____

____

____

____

____

Day 7

Is It Wrong to Doubt Your Faith?

And you will seek Me and find Me when you search
for Me with all your heart.

Jeremiah 29:13

Do you ever wonder if God truly exists or doubt that the stories in the Bible really took place? You might have these doubts because God doesn't seem to answer your prayers, or perhaps the dramatic stories in Scripture seem unrealistic. Maybe you feel ashamed to admit that you wrestle with these questions.

I have good news for you today. Asking questions, testing your faith, and working through your doubts are healthy parts of spiritual growth. Most importantly, God isn't mad at you or disappointed in you for asking difficult questions. He's not upset with you when you doubt him or have trouble making sense of the Bible.

God wants you to develop a faith that is your own. Working through doubts and hard questions are important parts of growing in your faith.

When you were younger, you were probably guided into your faith by your parents or another influential adult. However, as you grow toward adulthood, God will invite you into a faith that isn't merely your parents' faith. It is your own.

Part of stepping into your own beliefs involves sorting through difficult questions, wrestling with uncertainties, and deciding what you believe about the Bible's teachings. Working through these issues involves learning to read and study the Bible for yourself, seeking trustworthy Bible teachers to guide you, discovering how to discern God's voice through prayer, and engaging in honest conversations with more mature believers.

As a teenager, I had a difficult time accepting that Jesus was the only way to access God and eternity in heaven. At times, I wondered whether God was real or whether I merely *wanted* to believe that he was real. Some of the stories in the Bible seemed so outlandish (Noah's ark, Jonah and the fish, and more) that I wondered if the Bible was just a book of folktales designed to teach moral lessons.

Instead of being ashamed of my doubts, I worked through them. I sought answers, studied, listened to messages from trustworthy teachers, read books, and talked to mentors. Over time, God revealed himself to me in so many life-changing ways that I no longer doubted his existence.

Jesus has captured my heart. I sincerely believe that he is the way, the truth, and the life. Through experience, I have learned that the Bible is God's Living Word. I believe that every word is true and holds the power to transform my life from the inside out.

I challenge you to be honest about your doubts and questions. This is a vital part of stepping into your own faith and owning your beliefs.

Teen's Reflection

Do you doubt any aspects of your faith? Describe any questions you are currently wrestling with. What parts of the Bible are hard for you to believe or accept?

____

____

____

____

____

____

____

____

Mom's Reflection

Take the time to prayerfully read your daughter's reflection. There is no need to be threatened by her doubts. In fact, you might have some of the same questions and doubts. That's okay. Use this time to dig into God's Word, study, and seek wise counsel from others. Reassure your daughter that it is healthy to have doubts and questions. Assure her that you still do not have every answer. Then, aim to answer her questions as well as you can. If you don't have answers, consider studying God's Word together in pursuit of answers.

Day 8

Walking Through the Fire

He responded, "Look! I see four men
untied and walking about in the middle of the
fire unharmed, and the appearance of the fourth is
like a son of the gods!"

Daniel 3:25

Have you ever experienced a situation so difficult that it felt like you were walking through a fire? Maybe you've experienced the loss of a friend or loved one, or you're dealing with a long-term illness. Perhaps you often feel left out, stressed, or worried.

Sometimes, God uses the fires of life to burn away the parts of our lives that are holding us back. This process is always painful; however, it ultimately yields fruit in our lives and shapes us to look more like Jesus. Psalm 66:10 reads, "For You have tested us, O God; You have refined us as silver is refined."

In today's Focus Verse, three men named Shadrach, Meshach, and Abednego, had been thrown into a fiery furnace. These three men refused to worship a golden image their king had made. Miraculously, all three men emerged from the fire unscathed. They didn't even smell like smoke.

The miracle of their survival is awesome. However, an additional phenomenon took place as they walked through the fire: There was a fourth man in the fire with them.

Most Bible teachers suggest that this fourth Man was the pre-incarnate Christ. Jesus didn't leave these men to suffer in the fire alone. He went with them.

This truth has carried me through the darkest days of my life. It can carry you through the most difficult fires of your life as well.

Throughout the past decade, I have endured debilitating sickness. At times, my illness was so severe that I couldn't leave home for months. During those times, family members cared for me, and I often felt like giving up. I dealt with suicidal thoughts and deep depression.

On the darkest days, one truth carried me: I knew that Jesus was with me in my suffering.

I was so sick that it rarely *felt* like he was with me. Nevertheless, I trusted in the promise that he would never leave me (Hebrews 13:5), and I clung to that promise when I felt alone and hopeless.

Jesus wants you to know that he is with you in the fires you are facing today. He will never leave your side. He loves you so much that he already paid the price for every sin you have ever committed and every sin you will ever commit (Romans 5:8).

You might not feel his presence with you today, but that doesn't mean he has abandoned you. He is with you, and he will give you the strength to endure every fire you face in this lifetime.

Teen's Reflection

What is the most difficult "fire" you have ever experienced in your life? Describe your experience. Did you have a sense of Jesus' presence with you? In what way did your experience lead you closer to God or cause you to drift away from God? Describe any fires you are facing right now.

____

____

____

____

____

____

____

____

____

____

____

____

____

Mom's Reflection

After reflecting on your daughter's response, prayerfully share what you have learned about trusting Jesus in life's fires. Describe a time when you walked through a refining fire and had a difficult time sensing Jesus' presence. In what ways did God carry you through the difficult time? How did he support you and help you through it? What did you learn through it?

Day 9

Teen to Teen With Bekah

Comparing Yourself to Others

But the Lord said to Samuel, "Do not look at his appearance or at the height of his stature, because I have rejected him; for God does not see as man sees, since man looks at the outward appearance, but the Lord looks at the heart."

1 Samuel 16:7

Sometimes, I see images of models online or on TV and compare myself to them. These women are usually thin with big lips and small, button noses.

I know it's ridiculous to compare myself to them, but it's hard not to. When I catch myself wishing I looked like these models, I remind myself that God designed me to be the way I am for a reason.

God gave you unique features, too. You might feel like you have to look a certain way to be beautiful, but this isn't true! Maybe you don't like your freckles, your hair, or your nose. You might feel insecure about the shape or size of your body.

Most of us face self-critical thoughts at times. When these thoughts come to mind, remind yourself that God made you just the way you are for a specific reason.

You are unique for a purpose. If we all had the same features, this world would be a boring place. Everyone would look the same, and there would be no diversity. God wants you to embrace the way he made you.

Some teens try to cope with self-critical thoughts by starving themselves, working out too much, wearing lots of makeup, or dressing really stylish to make up for what feels lacking. This is tempting.

Sadly, when we go to extreme measures to change the way we look, we often hurt ourselves. Depriving ourselves of food or exercising too much can hurt our bodies. Wearing lots of makeup or expensive clothes might make us feel good about ourselves, but God is more concerned about what's on the inside than what's on the outside.

Instead of comparing ourselves to others, what if we worked on our hearts? Imagine how different the world would be if we stopped focusing on outward appearances and tried to be more loving, kind, caring, and thoughtful!

Teen's Reflection

Do you ever compare yourself to others and feel insecure? How do you try to compensate for these insecurities? In what ways would your life be different if you no longer felt insecure about your body?

____

____

____

____

____

____

____

____

____

____

____

Mom's Reflection

After prayerfully responding to your daughter's reflection, share one or two of your insecurities—past or present. Assure her that it's normal to compare ourselves to others, but it's best not to let these comparisons drive us to extreme insecurity or self-doubt. What have you learned about overcoming feelings of insecurity?

____

____

____

____

____

____

____

____

____

____

Day 10

How to Set Your Standards for Dating

Do not be mismatched with unbelievers; for what do righteousness and lawlessness share together, or what does light have in common with darkness?

2 Corinthians 6:14

When it comes to dating, what characteristics are most important to you? As a teen, my qualifications for potential boyfriends included good looks, a sense of humor, intelligence, and popularity.

Do you notice anything missing from my list?

Sadly, I wasn't overly concerned about faith, moral standards, or even how I was treated.

Looking back, it's clear to me now that my list was shallow and superficial. Instead of looking at the heart, I mostly focused on external characteristics.

Eventually, God showed me what was more important than outward appearances. I realized that I wanted to date guys who loved Jesus, treated me honorably, and shared my morals and values.

If you've never stepped back to consider what you're looking for in potential dating relationships, today is a good day to do so.

Consider the most important values and convictions in your life. Set a standard that you won't date anyone whose standards and foundational beliefs don't align with yours.

I encourage you to make it a priority to only date guys who love Jesus. This, in itself, will help you find guys whose morals and values are similar to yours. Here are some more questions to ask yourself when you consider your standards for dating:

How does this person treat others? Is he kind to all people?

Does his work ethic align with mine?

Do we share many interests?

Will he pressure me to cross physical boundaries I might not want to cross?

Do our personalities complement each other, and do we sincerely enjoy spending time together?

Are our values, core beliefs, and moral standards similar?

How do I feel when I'm with him? Do I feel like I can be myself?

It's tempting to focus on outward appearances when dating. Remember that all of these traits are subject to change. Furthermore, it's possible to be attractive, popular, and intelligent and also be self-centered, unkind, and ungodly.

Teen's Reflection

What characteristics do you look for when considering whether to date someone? After reading today's devotion, write down at least five traits you would like to prioritize when deciding whether or not to date someone in the future.

Mom's Reflection

Share anything you feel led to share about your dating experiences.   What mistakes have you made?   What characteristics do you consider important when dating? What would you tell your teenage self about dating with discretion?

Day 11

Swearing, Sex, and Violence

Finally, brothers and sisters, whatever is true, whatever is honorable, whatever is right, whatever is pure, whatever is lovely, whatever is commendable, if there is any excellence and if anything worthy of praise, think about these things.

Philippians 4:8

Not long ago, a friend told me about a show she'd been watching online. The plotline sounded entertaining, so I decided to check it out.

As I sat on the couch with eager expectations, I wasn't prepared for the opening scene. It showed a gruesome murder so vile that I had to look away from the TV.

Okay, maybe they're just trying to catch our attention. I'll give the first ten minutes a chance, I thought.

As I continued watching, the language was terrible. Sexual undertones were pervasive, and the overall tone was dark and disturbing.

Part of me felt compelled to keep watching because I wanted to see what happened. Meanwhile, I sensed the Holy Spirit whispering, *You know what you need to do.*

Obediently—although slightly begrudgingly—I turned it off and watched something different.

I wonder if you can relate. While watching a movie, scrolling online, or playing a video game, have you ever sensed the Spirit of God prompting you to turn it off or walk away?

It's not easy to walk away from a social media feed, TV show, or movie you sincerely enjoy. When your friends are into it, the fear of missing out adds an extra layer of curiosity.

I get it.

I felt awkward when my friend asked if I liked the show. I did my best not to sound judgmental or preachy, but I was honest and told her that it was just too violent and dark for me.

I've learned that when I ignore the promptings of the Holy Spirit in these situations, two things happen. First, my heart hardens. It becomes more difficult to discern God's voice in other areas of my life. Second, when I ignore the Holy Spirit's promptings, I become desensitized to entertainment that isn't honoring to God. This always pulls me away from God until I recognize it, repent, and return to God.

It's not easy, but God wants you to follow his guidance when it comes to entertainment. He isn't trying to steal your fun; he is protecting your heart and mind.

Teen's Reflection

Have you ever sensed that God wanted you to turn away from a movie, show, video game, or some other form of entertainment? How did you respond? Take a few minutes to reflect on your entertainment choices. Ask God to show you if you have become desensitized to anything that dishonors him. What is he showing you?

____

____

____

____

____

____

____

____

____

____

____

____

____

____

____

Mom's Reflection

Describe a time when you sensed the Holy Spirit leading you to turn away from an ungodly form of entertainment. How did you respond? Do you have any standards to protect yourself from engaging in media that doesn't honor God? Share any experiences or wisdom that might help your daughter make wise choices in this area.

____

____

____

Day 12

Teen to Teen With Bekah

How to Handle Drama

Love is patient, love is kind, it is not jealous; love does
not brag, it is not arrogant. It does not act
disgracefully, it does not seek its own benefit; it is not
provoked, does not keep an account of a
wrong suffered.

1 Corinthians 13:4-5

Let's imagine a scenario. You're hanging out with a close
friend. You've been friends for a couple of years, but she's
recently started being mean. She's been rolling her eyes
when you talk, correcting everything you say, and talking
about you behind your back.

There is no apparent reason why she's doing this. She
almost seems to be doing it for fun.

Frustrating, right?!

When this happens, I've learned several ways to deal
with it.

First, I remind myself that when friends are mean or
dramatic for no apparent reason, it's usually not about me.

It's typically because of something that's going on inside of them.

If you are dealing with a moody, mean friend, she's probably going through something internally, or she might be dealing with a tough situation at home. She might be trying to find an outlet for her painful emotions and has decided to be rude to you.

The second thing I remember is to do my best to be kind, rather than getting sucked into the drama. Being kind is vital in moments like these.

Let's talk about what might happen if you're not kind.

Imagine a friend starts a small argument at lunch. Later in the day, you both realize that she was right about the topic of discussion. At the end of the day, she walks up to you, points her finger at you, and says in a snarky voice, "I told you so!"

You fire back with something along the lines of, "I don't care! Stop being so mean about it! You're so self-absorbed it's hilarious! Leave me alone. You're so annoying!"

Now, she's hurt. By responding negatively, you're only feeding into the drama. Ironically, this might be exactly what your friend is expecting or hoping for.

Now, imagine you show kindness when she's snarky. You respond, "Oh, I guess you're right!" You let it drop and leave it at that.

This response might not make you feel better, but it's much healthier for both of you. Learning not to feed into drama will help all of your relationships.

The third thing I remember in times like these is the importance of boundaries. It's hard to be tossed around by a friend who is rude every day. When this happens, it's healthy to have a serious conversation with your friend and set some boundaries. These boundaries might include making it clear that you are not going to engage in arguments or respond to off-handed comments. If your friend doesn't respect these boundaries and keeps pushing you, it might be best to quietly step back from the friendship for a while.

Stepping back can be tough, but it can also be healthy. My mom used to explain it to me as opening my hand and letting a friend choose to distance herself from me. The friendship might one day recover; however, forcing it or holding on too tightly is never healthy.

I hope you're not dealing with friendship drama today. If you are—or the next time you experience it—these insights can help you respond in a godly way.

Have you ever dealt with a friend who was consistently mean to you? How did you respond? Are you facing any conflicts within your friendships right now? Describe what's going on.

____

____

____

____

____

____

____

____

____

____

____

____

____

____

Mom's Reflection

After offering your daughter practical ideas for dealing with friendship drama, write about a time when you had to face conflict within a friendship. Today, we explored three insights for handling conflict and drama. Can you add any additional insights to this list?

____

____

____

____

____

____

Day 13

Your Example Matters

Therefore, whether you eat or drink, or whatever you
do, do all things for the glory of God.

1 Corinthians 10:31

When I was a teenager, I used to sneak into the woods with
my friends and smoke cigarettes. Smoking was thrilling
because we knew we were doing something we shouldn't be
doing.

Let me pause right here and clarify that I'm *not* telling
you to go light a cigarette behind the garage. Please don't.
Smoking is an addictive habit, and it can ruin your lungs
and ruin your life. I'd also like to note that some of the
temptations I faced as a teen were slightly different than
the temptations you are probably facing. I recognize this,
but I share the cigarette example because we all face
temptations to indulge in behaviors that aren't good for us.

When I was a teenager, I wasn't worried about my lungs,
and I believed I was invincible. I didn't think I could
possibly become addicted to anything or mess up my life,
and I didn't always make the best decisions.

I'd been intermittently sneaking around and smoking
with my friends for quite a while when I invited my friend

Mary to head into the woods and smoke with me one dusky winter evening. Mary's response changed my life.

I could tell she was uncomfortable, but Mary stood her ground.

In a way that was kind but firm, Mary told me that she had never smoked and had no intentions of *ever* smoking.

I was caught off-guard. Instead of feeling cool, I suddenly felt like a bad influence, and I was ashamed of myself. I knew God had called me to encourage people and inspire them to live for him, yet I was pressuring my friend to lower her standards.

Later that night, after Mary went home, I buried my pack of cigarettes in the woods behind the house and decided I would never smoke again.

Mary taught me an important lesson that night. Her example motivated me to rise to a higher standard of living. She reminded me that I was called to set an example for others. Pressuring my friends to partake in ungodly behaviors was the exact opposite of the leadership God was seeking from me.

God is calling you to set an example for others, too. Are you leading them closer to him or leading them away from him?

Take some time to talk to God about the patterns in your life. Ask him to show you if you are setting a godly or ungodly example for others to follow. What is he showing you?

____

____

____

____

____

____

____

____

____

____

____

____

____

____

____

____

____

Mom's Reflection

After responding to your daughter's reflection, write about a time when you realized that your leadership was not pointing others to Christ. This is a great opportunity to practice being vulnerable as you build trust with your daughter. What has God taught you about the example you set?

____

____

____

____

____

Day 14

Be a Joyful Giver

Then the people rejoiced because they had offered so
willingly, for they made their offering to
the Lord wholeheartedly, and King David also
rejoiced greatly.

1 Chronicles 29:9

I wasn't feeling well the other day, and I overheard my husband as he encouraged our son to check on me.

"Mom, can I get you anything?" four-year-old Aiden asked a few minutes later as I rested on the couch. He smiled at me warmly and gave me a big hug. I could tell that he was happy to help me, and my heart overflowed with gratitude.

Imagine how different this scene might have looked if Aiden had listened to his dad's advice but approached me with a grumpy attitude. It would have been clear that he didn't want to help me, and my feelings would have been hurt.

It's easy for us to forget that God also has feelings. When we're sullen about giving to others—whether we're giving our time, energy, or money—our grouchiness hurts God's heart.

Do you ever stomp around your house when your parents ask you to help with a chore like taking out the garbage, doing the laundry, or washing the dishes? Maybe they force you to shovel your elderly neighbor's snowy sidewalk, help a grandparent with yardwork, or watch your younger siblings.

You might feel tempted to be cranky when you're not in the mood to give to others. In these times, remind yourself that God loves a cheerful giver (2 Corinthians 9:7).

Today's Focus Verse describes the way God's people willingly contributed toward the construction of God's temple. They freely gave their time, energy, and financial resources to help with the process. As a result, the Lord was pleased.

We all face situations in which we don't feel joyful about the work set before us. In these situations, we can pray, "Lord, change my heart. Help me to be a joyful giver instead of a grumpy giver." Nobody enjoys being served by a grumpy giver, not even God.

Teen's Reflection

What is your least favorite daily task? Maybe you don't like a chore your parents have assigned to you. Perhaps you don't enjoy your job, or you might have an especially unreasonable teacher or coach. Write about the part of your life that is most difficult to approach with a positive attitude. What would it look like to undertake this task with more gratitude and less grumbling?

____

____

____

____

____

____

____

____

____

____

____

Mom's Reflection

We all face everyday tasks that are unpleasant. Share what God has taught you about giving thanks or having a positive attitude instead of grumbling as you undertake your most unpleasant daily tasks.

____

____

____

____

____

____

____

____

____

Day 15

The Need to Be Liked

But if it is disagreeable in your sight to serve
the Lord, choose for yourselves today whom you will
serve: whether the gods which your fathers served,
which were beyond the Euphrates River, or the gods
of the Amorites in whose land you are living; but as
for me and my house, we will serve the Lord.

Joshua 24:15

How important is it for other people to like you? I assure you that I'm asking this question with all the love in my heart. You see, I have a great desire to be liked by others.

In high school, my desire to be liked led me to act in ways that weren't true to my character or convictions. I remember making fun of a younger girl at school because one of my friends was making fun of her. I also remember going to parties where other kids were drinking and doing drugs because it was the cool thing to do.

God knows that we easily fall into the same behaviors as the people surrounding us. For this reason, the Bible frequently reminds us to be careful about the company we keep and tells us to keep our focus on God.

In today's Focus Verse, God's people were entering into the Promised Land. The inhabitants of the land were not followers of God. They worshiped false gods and had their own religious rituals. These rituals included sexual orgies as forms of worship, sacrificing their children in fires to their gods, and other despicable practices.

Joshua, the leader of God's people, challenged them to choose whether they would conform to the ways of the people living in the land or choose to serve the One True God. He made it clear that they could not do both.

In a similar way, we will all face situations in which we need to separate ourselves from the people surrounding us in order to honor God. Certain social circles might not accept us if we don't laugh at their inappropriate jokes, swear, smoke, drink, or make fun of others. We might not be accepted by the popular crowd if we refuse to bend our moral standards or if we refuse to party with them.

In these situations, God is calling us to choose whom we will serve. Will we bend our morals and serve other people, or will we choose to honor God at the risk of offending others?

As I've grown and matured, I've accepted that everyone won't like me, and *that is okay*. I've also discovered that living in line with God's Word brings the peace and freedom I long for. I don't have to be best friends with everyone. I am loved relentlessly by the King of Kings, and his love frees me to be true to my values—even when others don't understand or approve.

Teen's Reflection

Ask God to show you how the desire to be liked has influenced your decisions and shaped your life. What is God showing you? Is God asking you to separate yourself from any behaviors that don't honor him? Is he asking you to distance yourself from any groups of people who are pulling you away from him? Share anything that comes to mind.

____

____

____

____

____

____

____

____

____

____

____

____

____

____

Mom's Reflection

After encouraging your teen, write about a time when you sensed God calling you to step away from the crowd for the sake of honoring him. Was it difficult? What did God teach you through your obedience (or disobedience)?

____

____

____

____

____

Day 16

God's Tests

God left him alone only to test him, so that He might know everything that was in his heart.

2 Chronicles 32:31

About 10 years ago, I sensed that God was calling me to start writing professionally. I've always enjoyed writing, but this was different. I sensed that I was to use writing as a way to directly minister to other people and help them experience God's love.

I assumed this meant that God was immediately going to lead me to write a book and acquire a publishing contract with a traditional publishing company. I started working on a book, and six months later, I presented it to a handful of literary agents and publishers.

Sadly, no one wanted my book.

I felt disappointed, but I decided to keep writing, believing that God would soon open the right door for me to secure a publishing contract. I'll spare you the details. Let me just say that I spent the next decade writing "practice books" that were all rejected by publishing companies. To this day, I've written at least 15 practice books—books that will never be published.

Finally, after years of hard and hidden work, God opened the right door for me to begin publicly sharing my books and publishing them.

As I reflect on the years I spent writing practice books that will never see the light of day, I have a clear sense of God's purpose for those years of hidden writing: God was testing me. He was seeing whether I would keep going in the face of rejection, failure, and disappointment. He was building my tenacity and refining me. God also used those years to help me hone the craft of writing.

Today's Focus Verse says that God tested King Hezekiah to see what was in his heart. God doesn't tempt us to sin, but he does test us to see what's in our hearts. He is looking for followers who will stick with him when the going gets tough. He's looking for people who trust him when circumstances don't make sense. He's looking for people who don't quit in the face of discouragement.

You might be feeling tempted to give up in some area of your life right now. Maybe you're worn out, and you're ready to turn your back on God. It might feel like God has gone silent or abandoned you.

Remember this: God never abandons his children (Deuteronomy 31:6). He is fighting for you (Exodus 14:14). What feels like silence from God might be his way of testing you to see what's in your heart. Commit to sticking with him and pressing on by faith. I can personally attest to the glory that comes on the other side of the testing.

Teen's Reflection

Are any circumstances in your life confusing right now? Do you feel uncertain about any part of your life? Maybe you've been facing rejection in a certain area, or you feel like you're coming up short. Describe your situation below.

____

____

____

____

____

____

____

____

____

____

____

____

____

____

Mom's Reflection

After prayerfully responding to your daughter's thoughts, write about a time when God tested you. Maybe he asked you to wait for a long time for a dream to come to pass, or perhaps you faced repeated rejections and disappointments. What did God teach you through the period of testing?

____

____

____

____

____

Day 17

Send Someone Else

But Moses said to God, "Who am I, that I should go to Pharaoh, and that I should bring the sons of Israel out of Egypt?"

Exodus 3:11

Have you ever asked God to choose someone else? Maybe you had to give a presentation, and the idea of speaking in front of an audience made you want to throw up. You might have been assigned the role of standing at the foul line with an opportunity to tie the game with three seconds remaining. Perhaps you've been given the difficult task of sharing tragic news with a friend or family member. In these moments, most of us would prefer for God to pick someone else.

When I think of wanting God to pick someone else, I think of public speaking. Every time I stand in front of a crowd, I have butterflies in my stomach, and I sometimes tremble so severely that I need a podium to hold my notes.

When I consider today's Focus Verse, I think about the way I feel when I'm asked to speak publicly, and I understand Moses' trepidation. In the context of this verse, God has just told Moses that he will speak to Pharaoh—the king of Egypt—and lead millions of Hebrew people out of slavery.

Moses puts up quite the protest and begs God to send someone else. Much to Moses' disappointment, God doesn't relent. He agrees to send Moses' brother, Aaron, to help him speak, but he doesn't let Moses off the hook.

At some point in your life, you might ask God to send someone else. When this happens, remember Moses' story. Moses wasn't eloquent—he felt nervous and underqualified. Scholars have even suggested that Moses had a stutter or speech impediment that made him especially anxious about the idea of speaking to Pharaoh and leading God's people. Nonetheless, God doesn't choose us based on our eloquence or worldly qualifications. He looks for those who love him, and then he sends us assignments that feel way too big for us.

Our role is to trust that the same God who calls us will also provide for us. God used Moses to free millions of people from slavery.

How does he want to use you?

Teen's Reflection

Have you ever asked God to choose someone else to step into a challenging situation that was placed in front of you? Are you currently asking God to send someone else to complete any assignments in your life? What do you sense God showing you about his provision and his calling for you?

____

____

____

____

____

____

____

____

____

____

____

____

____

____

Mom's Reflection

After responding to your daughter's reflection, write about a time when you asked God to send someone else to complete a task that was placed in front of you. How did the experience turn out, and what did it teach you?

____

____

____

____

____

____

____

____

____

Day 18

Your Rules or God's Rules?

Have them construct a sanctuary for Me, so that I
may dwell among them.

Exodus 25:8

If you've ever read through the Old Testament, you know
that the Bible contains many specific instructions. For
example, when God told his people to build a sanctuary for
him, he offered very detailed instructions. Reading through
God's commands about the color of the curtains and the
measurements for the different parts of the sanctuary can
feel tiresome. Maybe you wonder why the Bible contains so
many tedious instructions and details.

One reason for these thorough directions was that God
was teaching his people to follow him explicitly. Most
human beings—in ancient times *and* today—are tempted to
devise their own rules, standards, and ways of living.

God's specific instructions regarding the tabernacle
remind us that God has called us to live according to his
standards. We are not to blur the lines or devise our own
rules.

Today's society encourages people to create their own
values and morals. Ultimately, when we devise our own

standards and ignore God's boundaries in Scripture, we step away from God's protection and provision. Instead of experiencing the freedom we crave, by moving away from God's protective boundaries, we experience pain, restlessness, and a lack of peace in life.

One of the best examples involves sexuality. The world tells us that sex outside of marriage is normal and acceptable. However, God's Word tells us that his design for sex is only within a marriage between one man and one woman. We can create our own rules for sex, but we will end up hurt if we step outside of God's protective limitations.

Another example involves the accumulation of money. The world tells us that more money will make us happier and encourages us to pursue wealth. God's Word tells us that the love of money is a root of all sorts of evil and teaches that we cannot serve both God and the pursuit of excessive wealth. Have you ever noticed that the wealthiest people in the world aren't typically the most joyful and peaceful people?

The Bible is filled with countercultural insights regarding everything from the food we eat to the way we treat other people. Through personal experience, I've learned that even though some of God's rules are difficult for me to embrace, these detailed instructions are always for my good and my protection. This is true in your life, too.

Teen's Reflection

Which of the Bible's rules are most difficult for you to embrace? Today, write about any questions you have regarding God's boundaries surrounding sexuality or other challenging moral issues. What part of the Bible bothers you?

____

____

____

____

____

____

____

____

____

____

____

____

____

____

____

Mom's Reflection

Carefully read and prayerfully respond to your daughter's thoughts today. This might be a good time to pull out your Bible and study God's Word and his purpose for his boundaries together. After responding to her thoughts, describe a time in your life when you did not adhere to God's protective boundaries and faced a painful consequence as a result. What did the experience teach you?

____

____

____

____

Day 19

Wrestling With God

Then he said, "Let me go, for the dawn is breaking." But he said, "I will not let you go unless you bless me."

Genesis 32:26

A few years ago, our family went through a difficult time, and I often felt like I was wrestling with God. Sorting through my emotions—all while trying to trust God—often felt like an exhausting wrestling match.

During that time, I often thought about Jacob's all-night wrestling match with God.

On the night Jacob wrestled with God, he was preparing to meet his twin brother, Esau. Twenty years earlier, Jacob had tricked Esau and stolen his inheritance. Knowing he would soon encounter his angry brother, Jacob was concerned that Esau would seek revenge.

I imagine Jacob looked to God for comfort and peace as he prepared to meet his brother; however, God didn't show up as his Comforter. Instead, God showed up looking more like an equally matched man, and he wrestled with Jacob throughout the night. Sometime during their wrestling match, God injured Jacob by touching his thigh.

God injured Jacob to humble him. He taught Jacob that dependence on him is always better than self-reliance and human strength. Once Jacob had been humbled, God changed Jacob's name. Instead of Jacob, meaning, "deceiver," he was identified as Israel, meaning, "contender with God."

God used the wrestling match to transform Jacob for good.

Looking back on my wrestling match with God, I see the ways God used the difficult time for good in my life as well. He taught me that he is trustworthy even when I don't understand his ways. He also showed me that when my heart is surrendered to him, nothing can stop his plans for me.

What do you need God to do for you today? Have you been asking him to bring you comfort, heal your heart, or restore a part of your life that's been shattered? Maybe you've been begging him to open a door of opportunity or help you reach a goal that's important to you.

I encourage you to keep wrestling with God as you face your uncertain circumstances. Some of life's greatest blessings only come when we are willing to wrestle long and hard with God first.

Wrestling with God might look like going somewhere quiet and telling God everything you're feeling and thinking regarding a difficult situation in your life. It includes asking God hard questions and asking him for wisdom and direction. When you wrestle with God, you probably feel angry, frustrated, hurt, and doubtful. You bring all of these emotions to God and don't hold back. You let him see it all and ask him to reveal himself to you.

Most of us have at least a few unanswered prayers. It's important to note that often, God doesn't give us the answers we hope for when we wrestle with him. Yet he is capable of lifting our burdens so that we walk away feeling lighter, even if our questions remain. Wrestling with God is all about developing deeper trust in him and has very little to do with receiving clear answers from him.

Teen's Reflection

Have you been wrestling with God about any unanswered prayers or difficult issues in your life lately? Have you ever wrestled with God in the past? Write about any part of your life that doesn't make sense right now. What might God want to show you as you wrestle with him?

____

____

Mom's Reflection

After responding to your daughter, write about a time when you wrestled with God. What did God reveal to you as you wrestled with him?

Day 20

Teen to Teen with Bekah

Don't Quit Too Soon

May the Lord direct your hearts to the love of God
and to the perseverance of Christ.

2 Thessalonians 3:5

It's good to stick with things. Let me explain. When I first started running cross country last year, it was in the summertime. I enjoyed it at first, but when school started at the end of the summer, it felt like too much. I was tired at the end of long days of school. Staying for two extra hours to run in the summer heat was miserable.

I started thinking about quitting. I also felt overwhelmed by the fact that I couldn't decide what to do. The indecision amplified my stress.

After a talk with my mom, I decided it was best to stick it out to the end. And guess what? All the stress that was coming from not knowing what to do went away. I ended up having a blast! I made so many memories with the team and really enjoyed it. I was so glad I didn't quit.

My point is this: If you ever feel like you won't be able to get through something, don't give up right away. If you quit too soon, you may miss out on a great experience. Wait it out and see what happens. If you still don't enjoy it after a few months, it might be time to think about changing directions. But don't quit too soon! Give it time. God might even show you that you have a real gift for whatever activity you're participating in.

If you're thinking of giving up today, here's my encouragement: Don't give up! You've got this! Stick with it and keep seeking God's direction in the process. He might just use this to change your life forever!

Teen's Reflection

Have you ever wanted to quit something that felt really hard (a difficult class, a sport, a club, a job, or school in general)? What have you learned about sticking with things and giving them time? Do you want to give up in any areas of your life right now?

____

____

____

____

____

____

____

____

____

____

____

____

____

____

____

Mom's Reflection

After encouraging your daughter and responding to her reflection, write about a time when you wanted to give up. How did the experience work out? Did you stick with it or give up? What did God teach you through the experience?

Day 21

God Hears You

From the end of the earth I call to You when my heart is faint; Lead me to the rock that is higher than I.

Psalm 61:2

Backpacking is one of my favorite activities. One of my best backpacking memories took place with a friend on a stormy summer evening. After hiking into the wilderness, we set up camp and went for a swim in the river beside our camping spot.

I had my Bible and planned to read by the river after our swim. As we climbed from the water, a thunderstorm emerged from behind the hills. I decided to read my Bible beneath the ledge of a rockface by the water. My friend hurried back to the cover of the tent.

As we waited for the storm to pass in our respective shelters, I pulled out my Bible. The words in front of me seemed to be written specifically for my stormy moment by the river.

My bookmark was placed at Psalm 97. The beginning of the Psalm included the following words: "The Lord reigns, may the earth rejoice; May the many islands be joyful.

Clouds and thick darkness surround Him; Righteousness and justice are the foundation of His throne" (Psalm 97:1-2).

It seemed as though God was speaking to me directly. He was showing me his glory and simultaneously revealing himself to me through his Word and his creation.

When the storm passed, I hurried to the tent to tell my friend about my divine encounter. Before I could speak, she said, "Listen to what I just read in my Bible!" Sure enough, she began reading the words of Psalm 97.

Years later, when I need to be reminded that God hears my prayers, I remember that stormy camping trip. I remind myself that God hears every cry of my heart. He doesn't always reveal himself through serendipitous encounters, but he hears his children.

You might wonder if God hears you. Maybe you feel like he has forgotten you. Don't lose heart.

He has not forgotten you, and he hears your cries.

He is waiting to reveal himself to you.

Teen's Reflection

Has God ever revealed himself to you through a seemingly coincidental encounter similar to the one I described? How do these encounters build our faith? Have you been crying

out to God and feeling like he doesn't hear you? What does
he want to show you about his love and care for you?

____

____

____

____

____

____

____

____

____

____

____

Mom's Reflection

After encouraging your daughter, write about a time when it seemed as though God didn't hear your prayers. Since that time, what have you learned about God's faithfulness?

____

____

____

____

____

____

____

____

____

____

____

Day 22

Ask for Wisdom

So give Your servant an understanding heart to judge Your people, to discern between good and evil. For who is capable of judging this great people of Yours?

1 Kings 3:9

If God promised to grant you one request, what would you ask him to do for you? Maybe you'd ask him for a billion dollars or ask him to make you famous. You might ask him to change something about your appearance, your family, or a difficult situation in your life.

When Solomon became king, God told him he could ask for anything, and it would be granted to him. Instead of asking for fame, riches, or honor, Solomon made an unexpected request: He asked for wisdom.

Let's read God's response to Solomon: "Behold, I have given you a wise and discerning heart, so that there has been no one like you before you, nor shall one like you arise after you. I have also given you what you have not asked, both riches and honor, so that there will not be any among the kings like you all your days" (1 Kings 3:12-13).

God was so pleased with Solomon's request that he granted him everything else he could ever want!

The lesson for us is clear: God wants us to ask for wisdom.

Shortly after surrendering my life to God in my early twenties, I read King Solomon's story. I thought about the many situations in which I'd love to have more wisdom, and I asked God to make me wise.

I still have a lot to learn about life, faith, and walking with God; however, as I reflect on the past two decades, I can identify many situations in which God answered my prayer and granted me his wisdom.

Throughout the past decades, God has imparted his supernatural wisdom more times than I can count. He has helped me to love younger women with his love and showed me how to create a safe place for them to share their hearts. God's wisdom has also guided my career and helped me to be a more loving mother, wife, daughter, and friend.

I would not call myself a wise woman, but I can identify many moments in my life in which God has granted me wisdom beyond my years.

Have you asked God for wisdom? Why not ask today?

Teen's Reflection

Asking for wisdom doesn't have to be a one-time event. We can ask God for wisdom when we face a variety of situations, and God promises to provide the wisdom we need (James 1:5). In what area of your life do you need God's wisdom today? Write about this situation.

____

____

____

____

____

Mom's Reflection

After reading your daughter's thoughts, ask God for wisdom. Then, respond to your daughter with the wisest and most Spirit-filled advice you can offer. You might also use this space to write about a time when God granted you supernatural wisdom and guidance in your life. What have you learned about the pursuit of wisdom?

____

____

____

____

____

____

Day 23

How to Pray All Day

Pray without ceasing.

1 Thessalonians 5:17

Does the command to pray without ceasing sound unrealistic or impossible to you? If so, I can relate. The first time I read today's Focus Verse, I thought, *There's no way I can follow through with this kind of prayer. I have too many obligations, and I'm not moving to a monastery any time soon.*

Over time, God showed me that praying all day isn't about isolating ourselves or moving to monasteries. It's more like living on two levels. On one level, we are going about the everyday activities that fill our lives. Meanwhile, on a higher level, we are aware that God is with us. We listen for his gentle whispers to guide us. We imagine his arms surrounding us as he comforts us. We thank him for the gifts that fill our days, often pausing to think of him and let his love wash over us.

It can also be helpful to set aside certain times for intentionally focusing on God throughout our days. This might include taking a moment to tell God something you love about him first thing every morning or while you eat breakfast. You might set a timer on your phone to remind you to pause and talk to God when you sit down to eat lunch or get home from school. You might set another timer for the evening and stop what you're doing to thank God for his love and kindness.

Years ago, my friend Megan and I started a club called the Pink Watch Club. We both bought pink watches and set them to beep daily at noon. Every day, we both paused at noon to pray a quick prayer acknowledging God and thanking him for his love. Eventually, more friends joined the Pink Watch Club, and we soon had a band of prayer warriors approaching God at the same time every day.

You might not be into pink watches, but I challenge you to wear something on your hand or wrist to remind you to pause and pray. I've been wearing an extra elastic hair tie on my wrist for a few months. The thin strip of black elastic reminds me to pause and look toward God throughout the day.

Ask God to give you a creative way to remind yourself to pause and talk to him more often throughout your days. You might set a timer on your phone, write yourself notes, or wear a special watch or piece of jewelry.

This would be a great activity to try together as mother and daughter. Bekah and I periodically set timers on our watches and pray for each other at certain times of the day.

Praying together in this way has unified us and brought us closer together as we have sought God together.

Teen's Reflection

What hinders you from praying more often? Write about your experience with prayer. Have you found ways to pray that work for you? Do you find prayer boring or comforting? What frustrates you about prayer?

____

____

____

____

____

____

____

____

____

____

Mom's Reflection

After encouraging your daughter, write about your experience with prayer. What methods of prayer have worked for you? When have you felt bored or frustrated with prayer? Be honest. This is a time to grow together and encourage your teen by showing the ways we all struggle with prayer at times.

Day 24

When Friends Hurt You

The Lord also restored the fortunes of Job when he prayed for his friends, and the Lord increased double all that Job had.

Job 42:10

Are you frustrated with any of your friends right now? Maybe your friends went out over the weekend and forgot to invite you. Or maybe you just went through something tough—like a breakup or family crisis—and none of your friends seemed to care.

It hurts when our friends aren't empathetic and lack compassion.

Throughout the book of Job, you'll notice that as Job's life fell apart all around him, his friends weren't exactly supportive. Instead of encouraging him, they told Job that he must have sinned to deserve the punishment he was receiving from the Lord.

Sadly, Job's friends were wrong. God wasn't punishing Job. Instead, he was allowing Job to experience a terrible trial without offering answers about why it was taking place.

If I were Job, I might have held a grudge against my unsympathetic friends. I might have decided to look for new friends—friends who would be more caring and supportive.

Job might have been feeling this way, too. Yet there's an interesting plot-twist in his story: God restored Job's fortunes *when he prayed for his friends.*

A few months ago, I read this verse and realized that I needed to forgive someone who wasn't compassionate toward me during a recent loss. Instead of ruminating over my friend's lack of sympathy, I prayed blessings over her and forgave her. I remembered that forgiveness is a choice we make and not something we feel. We'll talk more about forgiveness later in this book.

For now, I challenge you to think of a time when you were hurt by a friend. Follow Job's example and pray for this person. Remember that people hurt others out of their own pain. Instead of plotting retaliation or holding a grudge, pray that God will bless your friend. Pray this prayer every time your friend comes to mind. Over time, you will find that God both heals and softens your wounded heart.

As Bekah shared earlier in this book, it's also important to note that setting boundaries with friends who are consistently unkind can be healthy. If a friend repeatedly betrays you or intentionally hurts you, it might be time to pull back from the friendship. In the meantime, it's also important not to hold onto bitterness in your heart.

You can set healthy boundaries—which might include deciding not to hang out with a friend who is consistently hurtful—while also letting go of grudges and extending forgiveness.

Teen's Reflection

Have you been hurt by a friend? Describe this situation and use this space to sort through your emotions. Before you close this book for the day, take a few minutes to pray that God will bless the friend who hurt you and reveal his goodness to your friend. Pray this prayer every time angry thoughts come to mind. Over time, God can heal your heart and your friendship.

____

____

____

____

____

____

Mom's Reflection

After encouraging your daughter to continue praying blessings over friends who were hurtful in the past, describe a time when a friend hurt you. How did you cope with the situation? What did God teach you through it? What have you learned about praying for those who hurt you?

Day 25

Hide This in Your Heart

I have treasured Your word in my heart,
So that I may not sin against You.

Psalm 119:11

Can you sing the lyrics of your favorite song? I listened to lots of classic rock when I was younger, and I can still sing along with most of the songs by CCR, the Eagles, and my favorite bands.

Our minds are extraordinary when it comes to retaining information. For this reason, it's wise to be careful about what we store in our minds. The Bible repeatedly encourages us to hide Scripture in our hearts so that God's Word will guide our lives, protect us, and encourage us.

Today's Focus Verse tells us to treasure and hide God's Word in our hearts. When we do so, God uses his Word to give us strength in difficult situations.

I've memorized hundreds of verses over the years. As a result, God's Word has carried me through hundreds of difficult situations. Here are a few examples:

When I ran track in high school, I often repeated the words of Colossians 3:23 and reminded myself to put my whole heart into everything I did.

When my luggage was lost on a trip overseas, I encouraged myself with the words of Matthew 6:25, which reads, "For this reason I say to you, do not be worried about your life, as to what you will eat or what you will drink; nor for your body, as to what you will put on. Is life not more than food, and the body more than clothing?"

The morning I went into labor with our first child, I was afraid of the pain I would have to endure. I spent the day repeating the words of John 14:27, which reads, "Peace I leave you, My peace I give you; not as the world gives, do I give to you. Do not let your hearts be troubled, nor fearful."

In his letter to the Roman church, the Apostle Paul told the Romans not to be conformed to the world, but to be transformed by the renewing of their minds (Romans 12:2). God's Word is the primary tool he uses to renew our minds.

I encourage you to commit to the discipline of memorizing God's Word. Write verses on notecards and hang them where you will see them. Start a journal and write down the verses you have memorized. Buy a Bible verse coloring book or create your own artistic displays of God's Word. God's Word will transform your life.

Teen's Reflection

Describe your experience with reading and memorizing the Bible. What aspect of Bible reading or memorization is most challenging for you? What would you like to be different about your relationship with God's Word?

____

____

____

____

Mom's Reflection

After responding to your daughter, write about your life-long journey with the Bible. What methods for Bible study, reading, and memorization have been the most helpful to you? What tips can you offer your daughter for developing a more vibrant relationship with the Bible?

____

____

____

____

____

Day 26

God Goes Before You

Then Deborah said to Barak, "Arise! For this is the day on which the Lord has handed Sisera over to you; behold, the Lord has gone out before you."

Judges 4:14

When I'm feeling nervous about the future, I think of my friend Debbie. She often says, "God's already there, Stace." Debbie's words remind me that God is always with me, and he goes before me in every situation. Nothing surprises God. This helps calm my fears when the future feels uncertain or scary.

God goes before you, too. He sees the full span of your life, and he will never be caught off guard. We will all face crises in our lives. Many of us will face uncertain diagnoses, shattering losses, financial fallouts, and situations that feel like they might destroy us. When these times come, we can rest in the fact that God is with us, and he goes ahead of us.

I'm not sure if my friend Debbie was named after Deborah in the Bible, but these two women both remind me how to trust God in uncertain times.

Deborah was the only female judge in Israel and also the only judge to be called a prophet. Deborah was also a warrior. When enemy Canaanite troops advanced against Israel, Deborah called an Israelite warrior named Barak to confront the enemy.

Barak responded by telling Deborah that he would only go into battle if Deborah joined him (Judges 4:8). Deborah agreed, and God's people eventually won the battle against Sisera and his army.

Deborah encouraged Barak by reminding him that the Lord went before him. In the same way, we can encourage ourselves when uncertain situations arise. God goes before us and makes a way for us. He will never leave us. When we seek first his kingdom and his righteousness, he promises to provide everything we need (Matthew 6:33).

Are you facing an uncertain future today? Remember that God is already there. He cannot be surprised. He has promised to stay with you and help you.

Teen's Reflection

Do you need the reassurance that God has gone before you into any situation you're facing today? Write about this situation. When you're finished writing, ask God to show you anything he wants you to know about this situation. Spend a few minutes resting in the assurance that God is already there.

Mom's Reflection

After prayerfully responding to your daughter's reflection, write about a time when your future felt uncertain. Looking back, what did you learn about God's faithfulness through the situation?

Day 27

Your Weakness Is God's Platform

And He has said to me, "My grace is sufficient for you, for power is perfected in weakness." Most gladly, therefore, I will rather boast about my weaknesses, so that the power of Christ may dwell in me.

2 Corinthians 12:9

Are you feeling weak in any way today? If so, there is good news for you: God loves to demonstrate his power in our weakest moments. I have experienced this countless times in my life. Let me share a few examples.

I spent years leading teens on mission trips to various cities in the United States and even outside of the country. We often had to travel all night on airplanes and sit for many hours in stuffy vans. We tended to be sleep-deprived and hungry.

Interestingly, God often chose to make his power known in my weakest moments. Teen girls opened up to me about their most shameful secrets and the most painful parts of their lives on overnight flights, as we sat in cramped vans, and as we squeezed together on bunkbeds made from plywood in tiny huts. I learned that if I gave what I had—

the last of my energy amid long, grueling days—the Lord would use it.

I have also experienced this regarding emotional weakness. I've found that when I feel emotionally exhausted and weak, other people tend to open up to me about their troubles. It is as if they sense that I'm not perfect, which makes me a safe person with whom to share.

Years ago, I faced a health scare, and I wanted nothing more than to curl up into a ball and wait for my next round of test results. Meanwhile, I sensed that God wanted me to reach out to an acquaintance and tell her about my issue.

I resisted the nudge from God for several days. Eventually, it became so strong that I finally obeyed, invited her to join me on a walk, and opened up to her.

To my surprise, she shared that she had been through a similar experience years earlier. She was able to offer insight into my situation and encourage me.

God also provided an opportunity for me to share my faith with her while we walked. I told her that I didn't know why God was allowing the situation, but I was doing my best to keep trusting him with the outcome. This led to a long conversation about walking with God and learning to trust him.

Because I shared from a place of weakness and vulnerability, she was open to what I had to say. She told me that she had a bad experience with church when she was younger, but she thanked me for sharing my faith in love and kindness. I realized that she wouldn't have been receptive if I had not come to her in vulnerability and weakness.

This can be true for you as well.

Learn to embrace your weaknesses as God's platform for revealing his power. Share your faith from a place of vulnerability (which often feels weak) instead of perfection. God can draw hearts to Christ in your weakness. He makes his power known most perfectly when we come to the end of our strength.

Teen's Reflection

How do you typically act when you feel weak? Do you try to hide your weaknesses from others? When it comes to sharing your faith, why do you think people are more receptive to hearing about Christ from those who are vulnerable than from those who are trying to prove they're perfect?

____

____

Mom's Reflection

Describe a time when God revealed his power through your weakness. What have you learned about embracing weakness and vulnerability instead of pretending to be strong at all times?

Day 28

Run After God

Then it happened, when the Philistine came closer to meet David, that David ran quickly toward the battle line to meet the Philistine.

1 Samuel 17:48

The story of David and Goliath might be so familiar to you that you're tempted to skip today's devotion. I hope you'll bear with me while I attempt to summarize this story in two short paragraphs, and then we'll talk about a surprising way that this story applies to us today.

First, here's my summary of the story of David and the giant: Goliath was an exceptionally large Philistine soldier who approached the Israelite army with a proposition. If any Israelite soldier could defeat him, the Philistines would surrender and become Israel's slaves. If Goliath won, Israel would serve the Philistines.

The Israelites were too scared to fight Goliath; however, when young David heard about the situation, he volunteered to fight Goliath. Samuel, the prophet, had declared that David would become Israel's king, but David had not yet moved into his role as king. He was still a shepherd at the time of this event.

On the day of the fight, David ran to the battle line, struck Goliath in the head with a stone from his sling, and cut the giant's head off (they don't show that part in the cartoons). Israel won the battle, and David became a sudden hero.

We can learn many lessons from this story. First, just as David defeated Goliath, Jesus defeated Satan at the cross. We can stand in Jesus' victory when we face life's spiritual battles because Jesus won the war through his death and resurrection. Jesus can help us slay the "giants" in our lives—giants like addictions, habitual sin patterns, fear, doubt, worry, and discouragement.

Second, just as David went to battle in the name of the Lord, we should fight life's battles in the name of the Lord. God wants us to turn to him and rely on him to help us.

These are both great takeaways. In addition to these insights, I'd also like to look at an obscure verse hidden within this familiar story. We are told in 1 Samuel 17:48 that David *ran* to the battle line to fight Goliath.

David was probably a teenager when he fought Goliath. The Hebrew word used to describe David in 1 Samuel 16:11 is a word that indicates youth as well as being small and insignificant in appearance.

Imagine a small teenage boy running in front of the entire Israelite army and taking on the challenge to fight a man who was over nine feet tall (1 Samuel 17:4).

Perhaps there's a reason why David ran to the battle. Maybe he knew that if he walked, he would lose courage. The Bible doesn't tell us what David was thinking, but we can learn from his radical trust in God.

David trusted God to lead him to victory, and he ran to fight God's battle. In the same way, there are times in our lives when God calls us to follow him by running after him with our whole hearts.

In your life, this might look like walking away from a behavior that dishonors God (and not turning back), taking the first step toward a dream, forgiving someone, or telling someone you trust about a sin that's burdening you.

Have you been putting off an act of obedience? Rather than putting it off for one more day, why don't you run to it?

Teen's Reflection

Ask God to show you one area of your life in which he is calling you to run after him in obedience. What has been holding you back? What would it look like to run after God in this situation?

____

____

____

____

____

____

Mom's Reflection

After encouraging your daughter to run after God in the area she described above, write about a time when you sensed God calling you to run after him in some area of obedience. What did you learn about him as a result of your experience?

____

____

____

____

Day 29

Why Save Sex for Marriage?

Or do you not know that your body is a temple of the
Holy Spirit within you, whom you have from God,
and that you are not your own?

1 Corinthians 6:19

Brooke was 13 when she attended a Christian conference with her youth group and committed to remaining sexually pure until marriage. The conference leaders even distributed purity rings to those who committed to saving sex for marriage. Brooke proudly wore her ring to remind herself that she was going to remain pure.

Two years later, Brooke started dating a guy from her school named Brad. Brad was charming, and it didn't take long for him to sweep Brooke off her feet. Early in their relationship, Brooke told Brad about her commitment to purity, and he assured her that he would support and respect her commitment.

Several months into their relationship, Brooke and Brad were sure they'd get married one day. They loved each other. They'd also started pushing the limits physically, and they'd crossed almost every line.

One night, temptation got the best of them. They crossed the final line and had sex. Once the line was crossed, Brooke thought, *Well, it's too late now. I've broken my commitment. I might as well keep on breaking it.*

I've changed the names, but Brooke and Brad represent dozens of young people I've known throughout my life. Let's use their story as a starting point for a conversation about why God calls us to save sex for marriage.

God designed sex as a way for a husband and wife to unite with one another by physically becoming one flesh. Sex creates a bond that is meant to exist only within the covenant of marriage. Sadly, sex outside of marriage also creates a bond that ties souls together. When you have sex with someone who isn't your spouse, you create an attachment that will most likely hurt you both in the future. Breaking the bond that is formed by sex is always deeply painful.

When you have sex with multiple people outside of marriage, you create deep attachments to each of them. In the meantime, your ability to create lasting, safe attachments weakens with each sexual encounter. This means that if you have sex with lots of people before getting married, someday, when you do get married, bonding with your spouse through sex might be a challenge.

Let's look at how this applies to Brooke and Brad. If they don't get married, they have given a gift intended only to be exchanged between husbands and wives to the wrong partners. Even if they do get married, their decision to have sex before marriage might hurt them both. One of them might be more strongly convicted about the sin of premarital sex, which will most likely lead to division when one partner is repentant, and the other is not. This will be a difficult predicament to work through within their marriage.

What's the lesson for us today?

If you've already had sex, your future is not ruined. However, God is calling you to stop, repent, and commit to purity. He wants to forgive and restore you. Don't tell yourself that it's too late and you might as well continue having sex. It's never too late to turn away from sinful behavior.

If you haven't had sex, I encourage you to make a commitment to stay strong in your convictions. You *will* face temptation in this area. In the meantime, God has promised not to let you be tempted beyond what you can bear. He will help you remain pure.

What's your perspective on saving sex for marriage? Is this something that's important to you? Why or why not? Do you have a sense that many of your friends are having sex? Is this something that's commonly talked about? Do you feel pressure to have sex? Write about anything that comes to mind as you process these thoughts.

____

____

____

____

____

____

____

____

____

____

Mom's Reflection

After *gently* encouraging your daughter by responding to her reflection in an open, nonjudgmental way, write about anything God has taught you about the sacredness of sex. What do you wish you'd known about sex and purity as a teenager? Bear in mind that you don't have to air all of your baggage here, Mom. Ask God for wisdom and direction as you aim to share what will minister to your daughter's heart.

Day 30

Pray for Everything!

With every prayer and request, pray at all times in
the Spirit, and with this in view, be alert with
all perseverance and every request for all the saints.

Ephesians 6:18

Has God ever answered your prayers in a surprising or
miraculous way? While you think about it, I'll share my
most recent answer to prayer.

Every Tuesday, Bekah's friends come over for something
we call "Friends Night." (We really need a more creative
name for our group!)

On Friends Night, I read a devotion, we talk about it, and
we enjoy a craft or fun activity according to the evening's
theme. It's a great way to have fun together, strengthen
their friendships, and also grow closer to God in the process.

Last week, Bekah came to me three minutes before her
friends were supposed to arrive and said, "Mom, I have a
terrible stomachache."

"Are you going to throw up?" I asked.

"No. It just hurts," she answered.

I immediately reviewed everything she'd eaten and realized that she had a stomachache two nights earlier after eating the same dinner.

"It's probably from dinner—and that huge cup of coffee you made for yourself," I assured her. "Why don't you just relax on the couch, and we'll try to keep this evening low-key."

As her friends began arriving, the evening started with a really weird vibe. Everyone followed Bekah's lead and sat on the couch staring at the TV. It wasn't a great start to our night.

I immediately picked up my phone and texted my praying friends. Every week, about 10 of us meet to talk about life and pray together. We also text each other throughout the week when we need prayer. I quickly explained the situation and asked them to pray for Bekah's stomach and pray that the weird vibe would shift.

Within 20 minutes, Bekah felt fine, we'd turned off the TV, and we had a great night of talking and painting together. God had answered our prayers.

God is waiting to answer your prayers, too; however, there is a prerequisite to answered prayers. You have to ask!

Teen's Reflection

If you could pray one prayer and have the assurance that God would answer your prayer according to your hopes, what would you ask for? Ask God if he wants to show you anything about this desire. What is he revealing to you? What stops you from praying more consistently?

____

____

____

____

____

____

____

____

____

____

____

____

____

____

____

____

____

Mom's Reflection

Describe a time when God answered your prayer in a surprising or miraculous way. What did the experience teach you about God's faithfulness and the importance of prayer?

____

____

____

____

Day 31

Teen to Teen With Bekah

Starting Your Day With God

I shall be satisfied with your likeness when I awake.

Psalm 17:15

Starting the day with God sounds like a great idea, but this isn't always easy to put into practice when you're tired or in a hurry. Today, I have a few ideas to get you started.

First, you can pray every morning. Start by telling God what's on your mind or thanking him for something from the previous day. Ask him to help you through your day and pray about whatever is on your heart.

If you like to write, journaling can also be a good way to start the day. Keep a journal and talk to God by writing in it. Tell him all of your concerns, ask him questions, or just write down what you're thankful for.

A journal can be a perfect place to write out your prayers. When God answers, go back and write his answers. This is a great way to build your faith as you look back on God's response to your prayers.

If you'd rather read than write, you might start each day by reading a devotional book. There are hundreds out there, and they can help you interact with the Bible in a way that makes it applicable to your life.

Last but not least, you can simply read your Bible. The Bible can be hard to understand at times, so you might want to find a study Bible with a commentary or use an online reading plan that explains what you're reading. If you're not sure where to begin, start in Psalms or the Gospel of John.

If all this feels overwhelming, ask God to show you just one way you could connect with him each morning. You might spend a moment talking to him before you get out of bed. You might put your Bible beside your bed and read a few verses before you get ready for the day (or read the Verse of the Day on Biblegateway.com). If you ride the bus to school, take a devotional book with you or read from a Bible app on your way to school. Listening to worship music is also a good way to focus on God at the start of each day.

The most important thing to remember is that God loves you and wants to spend time with you. Start your day with him, and you will be more likely to look to him throughout the remainder of the day.

Teen's Reflection

Do you regularly connect with God in the mornings? What makes this challenging for you? What suggestion from this

devotion could you add to your morning routine as a way of
spending time with God before the day begins?

____

____

____

____

____

____

____

____

____

____

____

Mom's Reflection

After responding to your daughter, write about your
experience with connecting with God in the morning. Be
honest. Is this a practice that works for you? Over the
years, what has worked well for you? What hasn't worked?
What tips or suggestions can you offer?

Day 32

Stick With It

Let's not become discouraged in doing good, for in due time we will reap, if we do not become weary.

Galatians 6:9

New beginnings are exciting. New school years, new relationships, and new jobs often fill us with enthusiasm and hope.

Beginning well usually isn't too tough.

Finishing well is a different story.

My weekend jogs are a good illustration of this point. Almost every weekend, I go on a 10-mile jog through the farm country of western Pennsylvania. When I first start running, my steps are usually light, and I have to hold my body back to avoid running too fast.

Mile Eight is a different story. At this point, I turn onto our road and run past the neighbors' farm as the wind whips against me on the barren hilltop. I'm already tired, and it takes everything within me to keep my legs moving. The energy and enthusiasm I possessed an hour earlier are long gone.

In many ways, life is similar to a 10-mile jog. We set out on new adventures feeling energized and excited. As time passes, we eventually lose steam and even consider giving up.

Life is filled with opportunities to embark on new endeavors, but most of us will face times when these new endeavors lose their excitement. Joining the team sounds like a great idea until the second week of training camp when every muscle hurts, it's 110 degrees, and you're not sure you can take another step.

Volunteering to teach the class of cute little kids seems like a great way to make a positive impact on the world until a rowdy little boy throws a colossal tantrum, and you can't do a thing to stop him.

Getting a part-time job at your favorite restaurant seems like a fantastic idea until your boss hands you a pair of rubber gloves and tells you it's your turn to clean the restroom.

We all face times when we'd rather give up than follow through with our commitments. Today, I encourage you to stick with it when the going gets tough. I'm not telling you to stay in a relationship with someone who puts you down or stay at a job where you're being harassed or mistreated. More accurately, I'm encouraging you not to walk away just because you're tired.

Be the kind of person who sticks it out. This resilience and grit will serve you well now and in the future.

Teen's Reflection

Have you ever quit something because you got tired or bored and later regretted it? Are you feeling tempted to quit in any area of your life right now? What is God showing you? As a way of following God's guidance in this area, write down whatever you sense God is leading you to do. Return to these words every time you feel tempted to quit. Consider writing down the words of Galatians 6:9 and posting this verse in a place where you will see it daily. Let it serve as a reminder not to give up.

____

____

____

____

____

____

____

Mom's Reflection

What have you learned about not giving up? Have you ever prematurely given up and regretted it later? What wisdom can you pass on when it comes to sticking with commitments?

Day 33

Are You Too Casual With God?

And the anger of the Lord burned against Uzzah,
and God struck him down there for his irreverence;
and he died there by the ark of God.

2 Samuel 6:7

It has been said that human beings tend to misunderstand God's character and "make God in man's image" instead of remembering that we are made in God's image. God's ways are not our ways, and his thoughts are not our thoughts (Isaiah 55:8-9). Nowhere is this disparity more clearly displayed than in today's Focus Verse.

To understand this verse, we need to take a quick detour back to the book of Exodus and learn about the ark of the covenant. Let's go!

In the book of Exodus, God commanded Moses to oversee the construction of something called the ark of the covenant. This took place one year after the departure from Egypt. The ark was a wooden chest covered in gold. It contained the two stone tablets (with the Ten Commandments written on them), Aaron's rod, and a container of manna.

The ark carried the presence of God, and God spoke with Moses from between the two cherubim (winged beings that protected the ark) on the ark's cover. When transporting the ark, it was to be carried by Levites using poles (Exodus 25-40).

With that in mind, let's imagine the scene in today's Focus Verse: King David is leading his men as they move the ark from a place called Baale-Judah to Jerusalem. As they transport the ark on a cart that's being pulled by oxen, one of the oxen stumbles, and the ark nearly topples over. To steady the ark, a man named Uzzah reaches out and touches it. Immediately, the Lord strikes Uzzah, and he dies.

I don't know about you, but my initial reaction to this scene goes something like this: "Seriously, God? He was only trying to help!"

I've wrestled with this story for years because Uzzah had good intentions. Nonetheless, this isn't a story about good intentions. This is a story about God's holiness and our tendency to become too casual with God.

At the time when this event took place, God's people had become too relaxed with God. By allowing the ark to be pulled in a cart using oxen, they were disobeying God's command to honor the ark by having Levites carry it using poles. This might not seem like a big deal to us; however, in ancient Israel, honorable people were transported using poles that were carried by people. Objects were carried in oxen-drawn carts. By putting the ark on an oxen-led cart, God's people were disrespecting him and overlooking his holiness. They were too casual with God.

Many people are too casual with God today, too. We become too informal with God when we toss his name around like a catchphrase or use it as a curse word. We are too cavalier with God when we excuse ourselves for living in intentional disobedience to him and focus on his grace and not his holiness. We are too casual when we thoughtlessly sing worship songs while daydreaming—forgetting that we are standing before glory so great it could knock us dead in an instant.

I assure you that there's no judgment here. I need to continually examine my life to assure that I'm not treating God casually. I stumble in this area often. I also need the reminder that God is not like us. He is far bigger, far more brilliant, and perfect.

Have you become too relaxed with God? Have you forgotten that he is the King of the world and Creator of the universe? Take a moment to reflect on God's holiness today.

Teen's Reflection

After taking a moment to reflect on the holiness and purity of God, humbly ask him if you have become too casual with him. Have you made him out to be like a person instead of remembering his holiness and glory? How often do you imagine him sitting on his heavenly throne in brilliant glory when you worship him? Do you misuse his name or sin against him without regard for his holiness? What step does he want you to take as a way of honoring his holiness?

____

____

____

____

____

____

____

____

____

____

____

____

____

____

____

Mom's Reflection

After responding to your daughter, write about ways in which you have been too casual with God in the past or present. What do you do to remind yourself of God's purity and holiness?

____

____

____

____

____

____

____

Day 34

Modern-Day Idols

Then he took the gold from their hands, and fashioned it with an engraving tool and made it into a cast metal calf; and they said, "This is your god, Israel, who brought you up from the land of Egypt."

Exodus 32:4

When Moses climbed Mount Sinai to receive the Ten Commandments, he stayed on the mountain for 40 days. Meanwhile, the people down below grew restless.

"Dude, what's taking him so long?" somebody probably asked.

"I don't know, but maybe we better come up with a backup plan in case he doesn't make it off the mountain," someone else might have suggested.

"How about we collect as much gold jewelry as we can find, melt it down, and turn it into a god we can see in real life—unlike Moses' unseen God," someone might have proposed.

"Awesome! I'll tell Aaron to head up this project," someone possibly declared.

A few days later, the people were thrilled with their backup plan. They had created a golden calf to worship, and they danced around it in joyful adoration.

You probably don't live in a culture in which worshiping statues is common, and this whole scenario might seem ridiculous to you. For this reason, it's important to understand the context of today's Focus Verse. God's people were coming out of Egypt, a place where idols were regularly worshiped. The image of a bull represented strength and fertility, and it made sense to the people to create a physical object to worship.

Similarly, we all face the temptation to worship what we can see instead of worshiping God. We might not create golden farm animals, but we worship the security found in our bank accounts, the accumulation of material possessions, and the comfort we find when we escape into our phones.

Anything that replaces God in your life is an idol. Here are a few common examples of idols: excessively aiming to please people, pursuing popularity, trying to be perfect, watching too much TV, being overly attached to social media, and obsessively managing our images.

Many of these behaviors aren't wrong in moderation; yet when they become central in our lives, they can easily turn into modern-day golden calves.

It's not wrong to watch TV, use social media, or care about your appearance. In the meantime, God calls us to balance. What is God showing you about balance in your life?

Teen's Reflection

Ask God to show you if there are any idols in your life right now. Have you been excessively turning to something other than him for comfort? What is he showing you? Where do you tend to turn for comfort and consolation instead of turning to God?

____

____

____

____

____

____

Mom's Reflection

After responding to your daughter's thoughts, write about
any worldly objects or pursuits that have become idols in
your life. How do you guard yourself from embracing these
idols? What do you do to find balance?

____

____

____

____

Day 35

Regrets and Repentance

For the sorrow that is according to the will of God produces a repentance without regret, leading to salvation, but the sorrow of the world produces death.

2 Corinthians 7:10

When was the last time you did something that you later regretted? We all make mistakes. None of us are immune to messing up, and I've never met anyone who didn't have at least a few regrets. I have plenty, and you might, too.

Here's what I've learned about regrets: When our remorse leads to repentance, we grow. We become more godly, mature people.

Our regrets don't have to define our lives. When we realize we've messed up, God wants us to turn away from patterns of poor decision-making and turn toward him. This turning is called repentance.

When we repent, we not only admit that we were wrong, but we actually turn in a different direction. We turn away from ungodly behavior and turn toward God in obedience.

You might have some huge regrets today. Maybe you've been regularly lying to your parents, mistreating someone at school, partying with your friends, or pushing the physical limits with your boyfriend.

Most likely, you know what you're doing is wrong, but you're not sure how to change.

Ask God to help you. Ask him to show you someone you could talk to—someone who would help you without judging you. God wants to help you turn away from this behavior and turn toward him.

My teens and early twenties left me with many regrets. When I finally decided to change my ways, I told my mom that I wanted to change. Part of me was afraid that she'd judge me or reject me when I came clean about my ungodly lifestyle.

Instead, my mom looked into my eyes and said, "Stacey, I'll always be on your side. I'll always be here to help you. I'll never reject you. You can count on me."

Even now, my eyes fill with tears as I share this moment with you. We all need people in our lives who will love and support us unconditionally.

If you've made it this far in this book with your mom or mentor, you have found a safe and loving source of support. This is truly a gift—and not everyone possesses this gift. I invite you to share any regrets in the space below today. Bringing our regrets into the light with others is often the first step toward healing. God uses other people to help dispel shame, heal our hearts, and lead us toward freedom.

Teen's Reflection

What is your biggest regret right now? If nothing comes to mind, ask God to show you if you've been burying any regrets. It might not be a scandalous or socially unacceptable behavior. Your regret could be something as simple as talking about a friend behind her back, fighting with a sibling, or disrespecting a parent. Do you sense God calling you to repent of anything today? What's stopping you from turning away from this behavior and turning toward God?

____

____

____

____

____

____

____

Mom's Reflection

We are wading into deep waters of trust today. Remember that anything your daughter shares with you is a gift that has been entrusted to you as you prayerfully respond to her reflections. After responding and encouraging her (with no sense of condemnation and no lectures), write about a time when God called you to repentance. What is the difference between remorse and repentance?

____

____

____

____

____

____

____

____

____

Day 36

When Your Heart Is Hurting

The Lord is near to the brokenhearted
And saves those who are crushed in spirit.

Psalm 34:18

How do you typically respond when your heart is hurting? Do you numb yourself with entertainment, food, or something else? Maybe you ignore sadness and hope that it will go away in time. Perhaps you tend to get stuck in despair and struggle with depression.

I have responded to emotional pain in each of these ways at different times. I also have a habit of quickly trying to fix any situation that leads to grief or sadness. For example, when a pet dies, I go into overdrive as I make a plan to adopt a new pet. When a dream falls short, I hurry to craft a strategy to bring a different dream to life.

Regrettably, running from grief is not a healthy way to work through it or move toward healing. Instead of numbing ourselves, ignoring our emotions, or trying to fix our painful circumstances, we grow through emotional pain by acknowledging it. God wants to help us unburden our painful emotions by giving them to him. This happens as we identify and name our feelings, process them with compassion, and lift them to the Lord.

Are you hurting today?

If so, being honest about your feelings is the first step toward healing. Take time to identify and name your emotions.

Then, process your thoughts with God. Tell him everything you're feeling. He already knows; telling him will help *you* sort through your emotions. Writing in a journal might help you find clarity.

After sorting through your feelings, imagine lifting your painful situation to God. He wants to make your burden lighter. Ask him to comfort you and begin healing your heart. Find an encouraging Bible verse to memorize—a verse that brings you comfort.

Lastly, give it time. Most of us would rather run through grief than face it. Grieving a life-changing loss can require months or even years. If you lost a loved one, your heart might always ache. If you just broke up with a long-time boyfriend, you will most likely need to grieve for a while. (We'll talk more about breakups in our next devotion.)

As you walk through your sadness, remember that God loves you. He wants to be your source of strength and comfort.

Describe a difficult loss that hurt you deeply. Have you found healing? If not, what might be hindering you? If so, describe your journey toward healing.

____

____

____

____

____

____

____

____

____

____

____

Mom's Reflection

After prayerfully responding to your daughter's thoughts, share your personal experience with grief. Describe a tough loss and share how God carried you through it.

Day 37

How to Survive a Breakup

Do not fear, for I am with you; Do not be afraid, for I am your God. I will strengthen you, I will also help you, I will also uphold you with My righteous right hand.

Isaiah 41:10

It wasn't supposed to end like this. You were supposed to walk off into the sunset holding hands while butterflies fluttered overhead—or something like that.

Sadly, as you stare out the window with tears in your eyes, your reality looks nothing like you expected.

It's over.

A tiny flicker of hope clings to the possibility that you'll get back together. Meanwhile, in the deepest part of your heart, you sense it's over for good.

Breakups are nothing short of heartbreaking.

I've lived through plenty of breakups, and I've learned that getting over them takes time.

If you're walking through a breakup right now, here are some encouraging insights to help you get through it.

First, give yourself time. You'd probably love to snap your fingers and suddenly feel better, but breakups are difficult. Give yourself time to grieve this loss. My most difficult breakup was with a guy I'd dated for two years. It took close to a full year before I was truly over him.

When grieving any loss, grief usually comes in waves. You might be starting to feel better when, suddenly, something triggers your sadness, and you can barely get out of bed.

I encourage you to keep getting out of bed. Resist the urge to isolate yourself or spend weeks alone in your room crying. This leads to our second point.

After a breakup, use your time to connect with friends and pursue activities that bring you joy. Find reasons to laugh. Make time to enjoy the good things in your life. When I walked through breakups in the past, I forced myself to spend time hiking, traveling to new places, planning camping trips, and connecting with friends. These activities helped me remember that my life consisted of much more than the relationship that fell apart.

Lastly, remember that God can use this for good. You might feel like you want to die. You probably feel like you'll never love someone this much again. Nevertheless, you can trust that God can use this difficult loss for good. He can use it to help you support others when they go through similar situations. He wants to use it to deepen your capacity for empathy. I also encourage you to resist the urge to blame God for letting this happen. Instead of turning away from him with your broken heart, turn toward him.

He wants to heal you and comfort you.

Teen's Reflection

Have you ever endured a difficult breakup? What did you learn through the experience? If you've never been through a breakup, describe a time when a friend was distraught over this experience.

____

____

____

____

____

____

____

____

Mom's Reflection

After encouraging your daughter, write about a difficult breakup in your life. What did God teach you through it?

Day 38

Forgiveness Heals

For if you forgive other people for their offenses, your heavenly Father will also forgive you. But if you do not forgive other people, then your Father will not forgive your offenses.

Matthew 6:14-15

Imagine you confided in a friend and shared your darkest secret. Several months later, you discovered that your friend betrayed you by sharing your secret with everyone in your school.

Most likely, you would feel angry and hurt. Depending on the nature of the secret, you might even feel embarrassed.

I hope this has never happened to you; however, most of us will face betrayal from close friends and loved ones throughout our lives.

Today's Focus Verse offers a difficult command for times like these: God tells us that if we don't forgive others, he won't forgive us. Ouch.

When it comes to extending forgiveness, I've learned several valuable lessons. First, forgiveness is something we do, not something we feel. You probably don't feel like forgiving those who have wronged you. Forgive them anyway.

Second, someone once told me that forgiveness is letting another person "off the hook." When we let others off the hook, we no longer cling to the offense. In the process, we realize that we are set free as well.

Letting someone off the hook includes forgiving them all over again every time the offense comes to mind. I've had to forgive some people countless times. After ending one dating relationship, angry thoughts about my ex came to mind hundreds of times. This meant that I had to forgive him hundreds of times.

This leads to our third point: Forgiveness is not the same as reconciliation. In my case, I knew that God was *not* asking me to return to the relationship with the guy I needed to repeatedly forgive. God wanted me to stop holding onto resentment, but he was *not* leading me to return to the unhealthy relationship.

Forgiving someone who betrayed you does not mean that you have to trust the person again or restore the relationship. This is true for former friends who are unkind, ex-boyfriends, and anyone who is not trustworthy.

Furthermore, there are times when we need to forgive those who have not apologized or sought forgiveness. God wants us to forgive others because holding onto unforgiveness leads to bitterness, resentment, and hard, unhealthy hearts. God wants our hearts to be healthy. When we release others by extending forgiveness—even to those who will never ask us for forgiveness—God begins a work of healing in our hearts.

Teen's Reflection

Take a moment to ask God if you need to forgive anyone today. What is he showing you? What is holding you back from extending forgiveness? Write about this situation.

____

____

____

____

____

____

____

____

____

____

____

____

____

____

____

____

Mom's Reflection

After responding to your daughter's reflection, write about a time when God asked you to forgive someone who had hurt you—someone you didn't feel like forgiving. Describe the shift that took place in your heart when you let this person off the hook.

Day 39

Are You Ignoring God?

And this is love, that we walk according to His commandments. This is the commandment, just as you have heard from the beginning, that you are to walk in it.

2 John 1:6

Have you ever heard the phrase, "Delayed obedience is disobedience"? When I was a teenager, I fell into the habit of partying with my friends on the weekends. I knew God wanted me to change my behavior, but I was having fun and didn't want to change. Meanwhile, every time I went to a quiet place to pray, I sensed God asking me to obey him and quit partying.

Sadly, I waited years to obey God and surrender my life to him. I explained this to Bekah a few months ago, and she said, "You made big mistakes and turned out okay, so why should I avoid making those same big mistakes?"

With tears in my eyes, I responded, "God has forgiven me, healed me, and restored me, but the pain that followed my mistakes was terrible. God allowed natural consequences to take place, and some of those consequences totally broke me. I wouldn't wish that on anyone."

When we don't obey God, he often allows the natural consequences of our actions to humble and break us. He does this in love, drawing us back into his protective boundaries like a good Father. This process often involves a lot of pain and heartache. Over time, I've learned that when God convicts me of a behavior I need to change, the best thing to do is to obey him immediately. Delayed obedience is the same as disobedience, and when we disobey God, we sin.

What might delayed obedience look like in your life? Maybe you have a sense that God is asking you to walk away from a bad habit, tell a trusted adult about a dark secret that haunts you, change what you're looking at on your phone, break up with a boyfriend who is pulling you away from him, or reach out to a friend who is struggling.

Maybe you've been putting it off because you don't want to make the change, or it feels uncomfortable.

Let me be the first to say that I understand.

I've been there.

However, the sooner you obey, the sooner God will redirect your life in a positive direction. As I've shared several times in this book already, God doesn't call us to obedience to stop us from having fun. His guidance is *always* for our protection, joy, and well-being.

Ask God to show you any area of your life in which you've been living in deliberate disobedience to him. What is stopping you from following him with your whole heart? What would it look like for you to step into God's plan for your life today?

____

____

____

____

____

____

____

____

____

____

____

____

____

____

____

____

Mom's Reflection

After encouraging your daughter, write about a time when you put off obedience to God. How did your situation turn out, and what did you learn?

____

____

____

____

____

____

Day 40

Teen to Teen With Bekah

A Time to Start Over

The Lord's acts of mercy indeed do not end,

for His compassions do not fail.

They are new every morning;

great is Your faithfulness.

Lamentations 3:22-23

A few months ago, I entered a poster competition. I had to make a poster displaying a specific topic and try to make the best artwork for my age group. The poster would be judged against other posters in the county. Then, it would be judged against others in the same division. Last of all, it would be judged against other posters in the whole state.

The previous year, I won at all three levels, and I was determined to win again. I got to work and thought I would do something awesome by using a combination of paint and colored pencils.

Sadly, the poster turned out to be a total flop and looked ugly and messy. I wasn't happy with how it looked. I was really upset and didn't know what to do.

When my mom suggested the possibility of starting over, I cried and yelled and said I wouldn't give up on the first poster I'd started.

Things were not going well for me at all.

After I was done crying, I realized that it wasn't a bad idea to restart. I decided that restarting wasn't the same as giving up; in fact, starting over was being persistent—the exact opposite of quitting.

As I began my second attempt at the poster, I got a new piece of paper and used markers instead. The poster turned out pretty well, and I won on all three levels again!

It's important to realize that there's nothing wrong with starting over. This can apply to trying new sports, hobbies, or activities of all sorts. It even applies to our relationships. Sometimes, we need to apologize to our parents or friends and start over.

Also, remember that every day is a new day to begin again! Lamentations 3:23 reminds us that God's mercy and compassion are new every morning. No matter what happened yesterday, we get to start over with each new day!

Ask God if you need a fresh start in any area of your life. What is he showing you? What might it look like to go back to the beginning and try again?

____

____

____

____

____

Mom's Reflection

After responding to your daughter, write about a time when you realized you needed a fresh start. What did God teach you through the process of starting over?

____

____

____

____

____

____

Day 41

God Uses Broken People

Blessed be the God and Father of our Lord Jesus Christ, the Father of mercies and God of all comfort, who comforts us in all our affliction so that we will be able to comfort those who are in any affliction with the comfort with which we ourselves are comforted by God.

2 Corinthians 1:3-4

My early twenties were tumultuous. I was angry with God and decided to live for myself instead of living for him. After a few tough years, I realized I wasn't cultivating the life I wanted for myself. I returned to God with a humble heart and asked him to help me put my life back together.

When I first returned to the Lord, I felt disqualified from ministering to others. In the meantime, God began the restorative work of healing my heart. I also began to realize that God uses broken people to fulfill his purposes.

I remember sharing my feelings with an older friend who looked straight into my eyes and said, "Stacey, God will use the hard parts of your story to minister to others in powerful ways."

Decades later, I can attest that my friend was right. God has used the most painful parts of my story to minister to young women who are facing similar situations. In fact, the hard parts of my story are the precise reason some of the women in my life have decided to trust me.

Nobody wants to share their dirt with someone who is perfect. The women in my life know I've made mistakes. Because I'm willing to be honest about my life, they offer me the gift of transparency about their lives.

I share this humbly. I also share it to encourage every young woman who feels too broken to be used by God.

God uses broken vessels.

Today's Focus Verse tells us that God wants us to comfort others with the same comfort we first received from him.

God will use the hard parts of your story to comfort, encourage, and inspire others, too. Revelation 12:11 reminds us that we overcome the enemy by the blood of the Lamb and the word of our testimony. Your story matters, and God wants to use it—even the imperfect parts—to minister to others.

Teen's Reflection

What parts of your life feel too broken or messed up to be used by God? What is God showing you about his plans for you? What holds you back from believing that God will use you?

____

____

____

____

____

____

____

____

____

____

____

____

____

____

____

____

Mom's Reflection

After responding to your daughter and encouraging her,
write about a part of your life that once felt broken but was
later used by God to help others.

____

____

____

____

____

____

Day 42

One Thing God Will Never Do

Be strong and courageous, do not be afraid or in dread of them, for the Lord your God is the One who is going with you. He will not desert you or abandon you.

Deuteronomy 31:6

I spent much of my early twenties wondering if God had abandoned me. After a series of disappointments and heartaches—including shattered athletic dreams, a tough breakup, and a long list of mistakes—it seemed that God had turned his back on me.

In my pain, I decided that if God wasn't going to hold true to his promise to stay with me forever, I was going to ignore his boundaries and live according to my desires. I said to myself, *If God isn't going to stand by his promise to never leave me, I'm done living for him and am going to live by my own standards.*

This mindset led to some of the most painful years of my life. After several years, I realized I'd made a mess of my life. I humbly returned to God, committed to living according to his standards, and began pursuing him with my whole heart.

In the years that followed, I learned that God is always faithful to keep his promises. He allowed me to face unpleasant consequences as a result of my behavior, but he never walked away from me.

Since that time, I have also learned that trials are not signs that God has forsaken me. More often, challenges are indications that God's presence is very near.

It's wise to examine our hearts and lives when troubles come. We should ask ourselves hard questions about whether we're living in intentional areas of disobedience to God. Difficult times are not always God's form of discipline, but God does use discomfort to get our attention and gently correct us.

Once we've examined our hearts and been honest about our sins, we can remember that trials often come because we live in a fallen world, and Satan is always working to destroy lives.

Additionally, difficult times are often the vessels God uses to help us become more mature. In the same way that fire refines silver, life's struggles refine us. God's purpose is that we will emerge from these fires with greater character and maturity—looking more like Christ.

As I reflect on the difficulties I've faced over the past few years, I realize that these trials weren't indications that God had abandoned me. Rather, they were signs that he was helping me grow. God was using the tough times to mold my heart into the image of his Son.

Today, I encourage you to guard your heart against the lie that God has abandoned you in tough times. God promises that he will *never* abandon his children (Deuteronomy 31:6, Hebrews 13:5, Matthew 28:20). God is with you, and he can use every difficult situation for your good and his glory.

Teen's Reflection

Describe a time in the past when God used a difficult situation to help you grow and become more mature. If nothing comes to mind, ask God to reveal a memory of such a time. Are you facing any troubling situations right now? What is God showing you about his purpose for your current trials?

____

____

____

____

____

____

____

____

____

____

____

____

____

____

____

Mom's Reflection

After responding to your daughter, write about a time when God used challenging circumstances to help you become more mature and complete—more Christlike.

____

____

Day 43

The Purpose of Your Passions

For we are His workmanship, created in Christ Jesus
for good works, which God prepared beforehand so
that we would walk in them.

Ephesians 2:10

Do you have any hobbies? Maybe you play a sport, enjoy performing on stage, or find fulfillment through creating artwork. You might be into photography, reading, hiking, caring for animals, or cooking.

If you don't have any hobbies, I encourage you to explore different activities and try to find one. Hobbies are great ways to relieve stress, connect with others, and even draw near to God.

I've had many hobbies over the years. Throughout my life, spending time in nature has consistently been at the top of my list of favorite activities. I love hiking, backpacking, traveling to new places, climbing mountains, and pretty much anything that involves the outdoors.

God uses my love of nature for a variety of purposes. I've learned that sharing my love for the wilderness with others is a great way to make memories with loved ones. It's also a wonderful way to make new friends who enjoy nature.

Time in the woods also refreshes my soul and helps me connect with God. This interest is not only a gift that I can share with others, but it's also a gift that God offers to replenish me.

What do you enjoy doing for fun? God wants this activity to be an avenue through which you connect with others. When you are a part of a team, club, or group of like-minded people, God will naturally create opportunities for you to share your faith. You will most likely form lasting friendships based on your shared experiences, enabling you to share the love of Christ in ways that are natural and unforced.

Additionally, your interests are God's gifts to you. He wants you to enjoy these activities and help you connect with him in the process. In this way, your hobbies can become pathways for drawing near to God and experiencing his presence.

Teen's Reflection

Describe your hobbies. What do you enjoy doing for fun? In what ways might God want to use these interests to help you share his love with others? How do you typically feel after enjoying your favorite hobby? In what ways do your favorite hobbies revive and replenish you?

____

____

____

Mom's Reflection

After responding to your daughter, write about your favorite
hobbies. In what ways has God used these interests to help
you connect with others and share his love? In what ways
does God use your hobbies to refresh you?

____

____

____

____

____

____

____

____

Day 44

A Simple Way to Have More Joy

It is good to give thanks to the Lord
and to sing praises to Your name, Most High.

Psalm 92:1

When I was a teenager, I decided to start a gratitude journal. A friend told me that she had started counting God's gifts, and I loved the idea.

I was determined to fill my journal with multitudes of blessings. I worked on my list for a few months, but my enthusiasm eventually dwindled. I shoved the journal in a box and haven't seen it since.

Years later, God began to show me the power of gratitude. I began studying the science of the human brain and learned that giving thanks can actually change the structure of the matter in our brains. We can destroy old, unhealthy brain matter and replace it with new, healthy matter. Consistently giving thanks is one of the most powerful ways to rewire our brains for joy.

For this reason, I try to begin every day by thanking God for several blessings. Some days, I look outside and thank him for songbirds, wildflowers, or sunrises. On other days, I reflect on my life and thank him for blessings from previous days: unexpected visits with friends, work projects that went well, or hugs from my kids.

When giving thanks doesn't come easily, I return to a simple principle: I can always thank God for his love and his character. I can thank him for being kind, patient, compassionate, and loving.

God wants to increase your joy as well. By regularly giving thanks, you can become a more joyful person. Why not start today?

As you look around the room where you're sitting right now, maybe you can't find a single reason to give thanks. The Lord has an invitation for you: Stop looking at what is temporal and lift your eyes to him. Thank him for strengthening you and protecting you. Thank him for being trustworthy. Give thanks for the ways he helps you in seen and unseen ways.

By purposefully guiding our hearts into thanksgiving, a shift takes place within us. We align ourselves with the Lord, and he fills us with his joy. As the joy of the Lord fills our hearts, our capacity for spontaneous gratitude expands.

Do you want more joy in your life?

Spend a moment thanking God for his gifts every morning. Reflect on your life and thank him for the moments that blessed you. Look around you and thank him for the gifts of a warm house and food to eat. If you feel stuck, thank God for his character, his love, and his goodness.

Lastly, I challenge you to start a gratitude journal. Begin listing God's gifts to you and keep the journal going until it is full. It might take years to fill the pages; however, by the end of your journey, you will most likely find that giving thanks has changed your life.

Teen's Reflection

Would you describe yourself as a naturally joyful person? On a scale of one to ten (one being the lowest amount of joy, and ten being the highest), how joyful are you? What is God showing you about learning to live with greater joy?

____

____

____

____

____

____

____

____

____

____

____

____

____

____

____

Mom's Reflection

After responding to your daughter, write about ways that
you have learned to increase joy in your life. When you feel
down, what do you do to lift your head?

____

____

____

____

Day 45

Discerning God's Voice

But the wisdom from above is first pure, then peace-loving, gentle, reasonable, full of mercy and good fruits, impartial, free of hypocrisy.

James 3:17

Have you ever been certain that God was directing you, only to later fall on your face, questioning whether you ever really heard from him?

Most believers will experience this at some point in their lives. If this has happened to you, there are several reasons why you might have mistaken your desires for God's direction. You might have sensed that God was telling you to do something, but you didn't test the idea to see if it aligned with Scripture. Maybe you didn't seek advice from someone with more experience or consider whether the decision was wise.

I've also discovered that I often miss God's guidance when I'm emotionally passionate about a situation. When we're emotional about our circumstances, we need to proceed with extreme caution as we sense whispers from the Holy Spirit.

Many people get this wrong in romantic relationships. Led by their strong emotions, they ignore red flags and mistake their feelings for God's voice. They convince themselves that they need to stay in unhealthy relationships or marry people who aren't right for them because they are led by their emotions instead of being led by God.

Whether it's a romantic relationship, a cause over which you are extremely passionate, or a specific dream that you deeply desire, be cautious about what you believe God is saying in these situations. Our emotions can be easily perceived as God's quiet whisper.

Take your concern to an older, wiser person who has been following Christ for a long time. This person can help you sort through your emotions and consider how God might lead you to make a decision that honors him.

I experienced this as a teenager when I was reluctant to break up with a guy who didn't treat me well. I loved him deeply, which led me to believe that we could work things out. When I prayed about the situation, I believed that God was telling me to stay in the relationship.

Finally, after months of emotional distress and dozens of fights and tearful arguments, I went to my mom for advice. My wise mother gently pointed out some of the unhealthy patterns in the relationship, noted that she and my dad did not argue in the same ways, and offered advice that changed my life. She said, "The fact that you love him doesn't mean you're supposed to be with him."

A few weeks later, I ended the relationship. I realized that the voice telling me to stay in the relationship wasn't God's voice after all.

It was simply the voice of my strong emotions.

God wants to guide us and direct us. As you seek his direction, I encourage you to be cautious, especially in emotional situations. It's easy to mistake our strong emotions for God's voice.

Meanwhile, if you thought you heard from God but are no longer certain—don't be discouraged. God is bigger than your ability to hear from him. There is no mistake he can't use for his glory. There is no wrong path he can't make right. Do your best to follow wherever you sense him leading you today and trust that he will put you on the right path as you continue to seek him.

Teen's Reflection

Do you ever struggle to discern the difference between your desires and God's voice? Are you seeking direction from God in any areas of your life today? What do you sense the Lord is saying to you? Does this impression align with Scripture, wisdom, and common sense? What role are your emotions playing in the situation?

____

____

____

____

____

____

Mom's Reflection

After responding to your daughter, write about a time when you mistook your desires for God's voice. What did you learn through the experience? What have you learned about hearing God's voice since that time?

____

____

____

____

____

Day 46

Awkward Beginnings

Do not despise these small beginnings, for the Lord rejoices to see the work begin.

Zechariah 4:10, NLT

In most realms of life, I don't enjoy the awkwardness of new beginnings. Whether I'm starting a new job, showing up at a new friend's house, trying to write a new book, or even trying a new recipe, the beginning is almost always uncomfortable.

A few years ago, I told a friend I was having a hard time getting started on a new writing project. She smiled at me and said, "You don't have to begin well; you simply need to begin."

Her words have been encouraging me since that day. Every time I embark on a new endeavor that feels awkward or uncomfortable, I remind myself that I don't have to begin well. I simply need to begin.

Some of us hesitate to begin new ventures because we want to be perfect from the start. The problem with this thinking is simple: We aren't perfect. Growth happens when we begin imperfectly and leave room for development. If we never begin, we will never grow.

Have you been putting off a step of obedience because you are afraid of beginning poorly? Maybe you've been thinking of joining the choir, trying out for a team, reaching out to a new friend, volunteering in your community, or applying for your first job.

Remember that growth happens when you are willing to step into the awkward beginning and learn through experience. The world's greatest chefs didn't cook five-star meals on their first attempts. The famous athletes on TV were once unskilled and insignificant—with plenty of room for failure and growth. Every great book begins with a blank page and a single word. Every great song begins with a single note.

Don't fear the awkward beginning of the dream you feel called to pursue. You will most likely face failure along the way. In the meantime, you don't need to fear failure. Every failure is an opportunity to grow. Remind yourself that it's better to begin poorly than never to begin at all.

Teen's Reflection

Describe a time when starting something new felt awkward or uncomfortable. Have you been putting off a new beginning in any area of your life because it feels uncomfortable? What is God asking you to do regarding this endeavor today?

Mom's Reflection

After encouraging your daughter, write about a time when you felt uncomfortable stepping out in faith, but God later blessed it. What have you learned about awkward beginnings?

Day 47

The Full Plate of Your Life

But seek first His kingdom and His righteousness,
and all these things will be provided to you.

Matthew 6:33

I begin most days sitting beside a window with my Bible on my lap and a cup of coffee in my hand. Some days, I'm able to focus on the Bible, enjoy my coffee, and connect with God in revitalizing ways.

On other days, I'm so overwhelmed by my to-do list that focusing on God feels impossible. My mind wanders to weekly dinner menus, grocery lists, writing projects, and more. These are the days when the plate of my life feels full, and I wonder if I might suffocate beneath the many commitments.

You have your own version of a full plate. Take a moment to consider your "plate." Your plate is filled with everything you do throughout the average week: going to school, participating in afterschool activities, hanging out with friends, going to church, doing chores around the house, and more. Jesus is probably somewhere on your plate as well. He might be squeezed onto the corner where you keep church, your weekly Bible study group, and maybe even this book.

Let me begin by saying that I'm so glad Jesus is on your plate. This is a great start. Yet it's not the final destination.

You might expect me to challenge you to view Jesus as the main course on the plate of your life. Instead, I have a radical suggestion: Don't view Jesus as the main course on the plate of your life; rather, ask him to undergird every part of your life and remind yourself Jesus *is the plate* holding your world together. Jesus wants to be your foundation. He wants to be the uniting force upholding everything you undertake.

Scripture tells us that the most important command is to love God with all our strength. Have you ever wondered how to give God every ounce of your love while also loving your friends, family, and the many people in your life?

The image of a full plate can help us understand what it looks like to love God with our whole hearts while also loving the people He places in front of us. When a loving relationship with God is the foundation for our lives, we become his vessels. The love we pour onto others is no longer our own human love; it is the overflow of the love God has poured into us.

Here's the most beautiful aspect of this imagery: The more you love God, the greater your capacity for loving others will become. God wants to be the source of the love you carry to others. Make him the foundation of your life, and he will equip you to be his vessel of love to the world around you.

Teen's Reflection

Take a few minutes and envision a plate representing your life. What activities and commitments fill your plate? How does your perspective change when you imagine Jesus as the foundation for everything you do—the plate holding your world together? In what ways would your life be different if Jesus were the foundation upholding your entire life?

____

____

____

____

____

____

____

____

____

Mom's Reflection

After responding to your teen, write about the methods you use to remind yourself to stay centered on Christ, allowing him to be the foundation undergirding your life. What has he taught you about inviting him into every realm of your life?

Day 48

Teen to Teen With Bekah

You've Got This!

Yet those who wait for the Lord
will gain new strength.

Isaiah 40:31

A few years ago, my mom and I decided to end the year with an adventure. It was New Year's Eve, and we decided to walk five miles from our house to my grandma and grandpa's house.

We set out an hour before dark, and the air was damp and cold. Snow covered the farmland surrounding us.

We were less than half-way there when darkness started to fall. It was bitter cold, and we could see our breath in the chilly evening air.

My sore feet rubbed against my shoes causing large, painful blisters. We trudged on, imagining the taste of Grandma's warm, fresh, homemade chocolate chip cookies. After a lot of time and effort, we finally made it to their house!

In situations like this, endurance is vital. You might not have to endure a five-mile walk today, but you probably need to endure in some area of your life.

Maybe it feels like this school year will never end, and you're counting down the days until your next break. You might not have a happy life at home, or you might be dealing with a bully.

You might even feel like life is wounding you right now. If that's the case, remember that the wounds you feel now will one day heal. Don't give up. Keep walking.

I've learned that pressing toward the finish line is important. Sometimes, we feel tempted to give up when life gets hard, but it's important to try to finish what we start in life. If you started a sport and are becoming tired of it, try to finish the season. If the school year feels like it's dragging, just keep going. It will eventually end. It may seem rough now, but it will be worth it when you reach the end, whether it is a chocolate chip cookie or a greater goal.

Teen's Reflection

Which area of your life requires endurance right now? As you reflect on this, consider your ultimate goal. What goal are you pursuing? How does focusing on your goal help you keep pressing forward?

Mom's Reflection

After encouraging your daughter, write about a time when endurance paid off for you. What has God taught you about pressing through adversity?

Day 49

Be Gentle With Yourself

Let your gentle spirit be known to all people. The
Lord is near.

Philippians 4:5

I've spent most of my life being unreasonably hard on myself. I stand in front of mirrors, grab my love handles, and commit to more rigorous ab workouts. I regularly push myself beyond exhaustion and feel guilty for taking naps—even after staying up all night tending to my kids when they're sick. I tell myself to suck it up, try harder, go faster, and give more.

You might not push yourself through exhaustion or condemningly grab your belly fat when you stand in front of the mirror, but I imagine you know all about self-critical attitudes. Most of us would never talk to our friends the way we talk to ourselves.

Hopefully, you wouldn't slap your friend on the back and tell her to get over it the day after a crushing heartbreak. Hopefully, you don't tell your friends that they're fat, stupid, unlikeable, or awkward. However, in the quiet part of your mind, you might speak these words to yourself—and worse.

Not long ago, God showed me that the critical spirit with which I judge myself has a significant impact on the way I love others. Being self-critical will eventually lead me to be critical of others.

Jesus tells us to love our neighbors as we love ourselves. Meanwhile, if we're critical of ourselves, we will eventually project our critical spirits onto others as well.

Throughout the past few years, God has been teaching me to be gentle with myself. When I catch myself embracing self-critical thoughts or treating my body poorly, I think of my kids. I would never tell my kids that they're ugly or fat. I wouldn't shove junk food into their mouths to help them escape their emotions, and I wouldn't ask them to function after only minutes of sleep.

Instead of being critical, I'm learning to be thankful for these legs that have carried me thousands of miles, the lines on my face that show my age, and this body that regularly endures sleepless nights. I'm also learning to treat myself the way I treat my kids—with gentleness, kindness, and care.

I challenge you to think of a younger person you care about: a younger sibling, neighbor, relative, or someone you babysit. The next time you catch yourself embracing self-critical thoughts or treating your body with a lack of care, think of this child. If you wouldn't treat the child the way

you are treating yourself, then it's probably time to change
the way you're treating yourself.

Teen's Reflection

If you could change three things about yourself, what would
you change? What thoughts or behaviors would you change
if you started treating yourself the way you treat the most
precious child in your life? What is God showing you?

____

____

____

____

____

____

____

____

____

____

____

____

____

____

____

____

____

Mom's Reflection

After responding to your daughter, write about the parts of
yourself that you would like to change. What have you
learned about being critical of yourself?

____

____

____

____

Day 50

Finding Your Calling

And He said to him, "You shall love the Lord your God with all your heart, and with all your soul, and with all your mind." This is the great and foremost commandment. The second is like it, "You shall love your neighbor as yourself."

Matthew 22:37-39

I vividly remember the moment when I decided I wanted to be a teacher. It was my junior year of high school, and I was sitting on a grassy hillside as mist ascended from the valley below.

Sitting on the wet earth, I searched my life for the places that made me feel most alive, most filled with purpose.

I loved the woods and had always assumed I would follow a career path in wildlife biology.

Meanwhile, there was one passion that sparked a deeper sense of purpose. It evoked a sense that I was making a positive impact on the lives of others. I felt this sense of purpose most acutely when I was leading younger girls as a captain on my high school track and volleyball teams.

As I sat on the hillside, I asked God to show me what I ought to declare as my major for my undergraduate degree. Contrary to every part of my flesh, I sensed that I was to lay down my desire to work in the woods and commit my life to serving others. God showed me that a calling is about more than just passion; a calling is about using our passions to help others. That afternoon, I decided I wanted to become a teacher and coach.

Most likely, you're beginning to wonder what God might be calling you to do in the future. Here are two good questions to ask yourself: *Where do my passions and talents collide with a need God can use me to meet? While helping others in the past, when have I felt most alive and fulfilled, sensing that I was making an impact?*

Perhaps you enjoyed working with younger children at summer camp. You might love studying science and exploring creative ways to care for the earth. Maybe you enjoy solving problems, offering hospitality, or working with numbers.

Pay attention to the pursuits that create a sense of purpose and fulfillment. Ask God to show you how these interests could be used to help and serve others, and you'll be well on your way to finding your calling.

Lastly, I want to encourage you not to get too caught up in choosing the perfect career path or making the ideal future plan. God is more concerned about how you live than the job you choose.

Make your life about following God's two greatest commands—loving him and loving others—and he will direct you. He will also be pleased, whether you are working as a waitress or leading a multimillion-dollar business.

Many years after my moment on the hillside, I'm no longer a classroom teacher. This reminds me that the places where we live out our callings can change with time. Meanwhile, the primary focus of my calling remains: Wherever I go, I aim to love God and love others.

Teen's Reflection

Spend some time talking to God about your passions and talents. In what ways might God want to use these passions and talents to help others? Do you have a sense of direction for your future?

____

____

____

____

____

____

____

____

____

____

____

____

____

____

____

Mom's Reflection

After affirming your daughter's response, share any talents and passions you see in her life. Offer insight into how God might want to use these unique parts of her life for good in the world. What have you learned about finding God's calling in your life?

____

____

____

____

____

____

____

____

____

____

____

Before We Go

Congratulations! After reading and reflecting on these devotions, we hope you've grown closer to God and developed a closer relationship with one another.

We encourage you to keep the conversation going with one another and continue pursuing God, both individually and together. We are currently working on two more devotional books for teens. Watch for them to go on sale within the next year!

We also invite you to check out our other books. *Girl to Girl: 60 Mother-Daughter Devotions for a Closer Relationship and Deeper Faith* is our first mother-daughter devotional book. It is written for girls ages 7-17 and has transformed thousands of lives. Additionally, look for Stacey's life-changing book for women, *Lean Into Grace: Let God's Grace Heal Your Heart, Refresh Your Soul, and Set You Free.*

Last, we pray that God continues to bless you and shower his favor upon you as you seek him. He loves you relentlessly, and he will never stop pursuing you.

In Love,

Bekah and Stacey